Safe Practices in the Arts & Crafts

A Studio Guide

2nd Edition—1985
Julian A. Waller, M.D.,
M.P.H.
Published by
The College Art
Association of America

Copyright © 1978, 1985 by the College Art Association of America
Published 1985 in the United States of America

Library of Congress Cataloging in Publication Data

Main entry under title:
Safe practices in the arts and crafts
Includes appendixes: getting additional information
Waller, Julian A.
ISBN 0-9604826-1-X

College Art Association of America   149 Madison Avenue   New York, N.Y. 10016

Contents

Acknowledgments

This is the first revision of *Safe Practices in the Arts and Crafts: A Studio Guide* written by Gail Coningsby Barazani in 1978. Fundamental to both editions was Jerome Siedlecki's 1968 article in the *Journal of the American Medical Association,* which pointed out that many of the real or potential health hazards to artists that were identified by Bernardino Ramazzini in 1700 still exist today.

Few physicians paid attention to Siedlecki's warning. But among artists and some health professionals an effort began in the 1970s to find answers, to educate artists, health professionals, and suppliers of art materials, and to identify what is *not* a problem as well as what *is.* Among those contributing to that effort have been Dr. Bertram Carnow and his staff—including Gail Barazani—at the University of Illinois School of Public Health, Michael McCann and Monona Rossol of the Center for Occupational Hazards in New York (to whom I am particularly grateful for their extensive suggestions on this work), Bill Alexander, a potter, my colleague at the University of Vermont, Lawrence Whitehead, and, more recently, the health and safety staff of the School of the Art Institute of Chicago.

These groups and individuals have freely exchanged advice and resources among themselves and with the National Institute of Occupational Health and Safety (NIOSH), the Consumer Product Safety Commission (CPSC), and the public. Neither the original *Guide* nor this revision would have been possible without this cross-fertilization. Nor would the *Guide* have existed without the foresight and leadership of the College Art Association to deal forthrightly with a problem that both artists and the medical profession have ignored for far too long.

Although I am a physician, it was not my medical colleagues who alerted me to health issues for artists. Rather, it was the needs of my wife, who is a fiber artist, as well as those of our many friends who earn their livings and obtain pleasures in life as artists, that were instrumental in the development of this revision.

Finally, mention should be made of my teachers and fellow students at Haystack Mountain School of Crafts and the University of Vermont Art Department, all of whom have helped me over the past several years to test the theoretical and superficial solutions that physicians too often offer against the realities of the artist's working life. They showed me what can and cannot work in the press of production, in preparing for an imminent show, or in teaching or working with limited funds in an environment that was not originally designed for the activities of the artist and that sometimes the artist may not be permitted to alter. To all these individuals I am grateful.

Introduction: What this Guide Is—And What It Is Not

In order to achieve their aesthetic objectives artists must know how to use the tools of their trade. Often these materials and processes produce unexpected and unfortunate effects: a color may not be "true," it may fade with time, or a material may be hard to manipulate without breaking, crazing, or otherwise going bad. Guidebooks have been written to assist the artist in anticipating and avoiding these effects.

The purpose of this guidebook is to alert you to another group of unfortunate effects—those that may occur in the artist rather than in the work. These are potential problems of ill health that are associated with many—but not all—of the materials and processes. And, as with fading, some of these effects may not become apparent until several years have passed. *Knowing the health aspects of art materials and processes is as integral to being a successful artist as is knowing their other aspects.* I have received enough urgent phone calls from artists who have suddenly had to stop work because of illness while preparing for THE SHOW to make me urge that this statement not be taken lightly.

In order to know those health aspects one must learn some of the concepts and terminology used by chemists, physicians, and industrial hygienists. It is not the aim of this *Guide* to make you a specialist in these areas. If you were really interested in these fields, I assume you would have studied chemistry, medicine, or industrial hygiene instead of, or in addition to, art. The *Guide,* therefore, will offer the minimun information that is consistent with the necessary understanding.

The first section of the *Guide* discusses general principles and methods that will enable you to avoid potential health hazards even if you are unable to determine the specific characteristics of materials you are using. Then follows a brief section devoted to some of the specific problems in each of several mediums. Further information can be obtained from the references, and resource materials listed in the appendixes.

The *Guide* will try to suggest how to achieve safety at low cost. Many safe practices involve no expenditure of money at all, and very substantial improvements can usually be made thoughout an entire studio for a total outlay of less than $100.

It is not my intention to make you fearful; but health problems do exist and require preventive action. I shall not list specific symptoms, because most symptoms attributable to art work may also occur for reasons that are unrelated to artistic process. My experience has taught me that such lists simply create anxiety without really imparting knowledge. Since most physicians know relatively little about occupational medicine, I have included a chapter on how to deal with physicians.

Finally, the complete removal of all risks to health and safety is an unattainable ideal. Far more practical is to select those steps and activities that will reduce risks to an acceptable level while permitting continuation of artistic endeavor. Many ways of reducing risks are described in this *Guide.* If you are in generally good health you should be able to choose several nonintrusive methods that will be suitable to your needs. If you already have a health problem, it may be necessary to take more difficult or more expensive steps. Choose whatever methods meet your needs. Don't worry or feel guilty about those methods you haven't chosen. And get on with the work you want to do!

I Is there Really a Problem?

The effects of certain kinds of work upon health have been observed for thousands of years. The Egyptians recognized that gold miners died after a few years of work in the dust and found that hernias were a common hazard in pyramid-building operations. But it was not until the early 18th century that the medical profession turned its attention to health problems of the laboring class. In 1700 Bernardino Ramazzini published *De Morbis Artificum,* the first comprehensive study of the diseases common to practitioners of various trades.

One of the several artistic trades Ramazzini observed was that of painters, who worked in poorly ventilated rooms with complicated chemical mixtures. He attributed their poor health to contaminated air, dirty clothing, and inadequate diet. Although diet has probably improved, 20th-century artists still face many of the same problems, including those arising from contacts with the same chemicals that posed a hazard in Ramazzini's time.

But, in addition to those materials and processes that have remained the same, new ones have come along with their own sets of problems. These include photography, laser imaging, plastics and polyester resins, sandblasting, epoxies, and organic dyes, to mention a few. Many of these materials and processes have been developed and used only since the 1940s and 1950s, and their long-term health effects—or lack of effects—are only now becoming apparent.

Something else has changed as well. In the past half century education has expanded for the general population in the United States. Art courses are now available not only in elementary and high schools but also for the millions of people who attend college or adult-education programs. Additionally, people now have more leisure time, and many are devoting that time to avocational art. A 1975 Harris poll estimated that as many as one out of every four Americans works part time with art or craft processes.

With so many people exposed to new materials in the making of art, reports of health problems began occasionally to appear. In 1963, in *Art News,* for example, Robert Mallary, a New York sculptor, described a serious illness that resulted from his work with polyester resins, and he discussed adverse health effects of aerosol spray fixatives, including the death of an infant in a room where his artist-father was spraying. In some cases serious illness or even death has occurred to individuals with very minimal exposure.

To what extent do such reports indicate that more than a very occasional problem exists? Unfortunately, it is not possible to provide a firm answer. Large-scale studies of occupational illness such as those done for industry have never been done for artists. Thus, while it is possible to say that many artists are being exposed—and for more hours per week—to the same materials that have been identified in industrial studies as harmful, it is not possible to report what percentage of those artists will end up sick after ten or twenty years of such exposure.

Only two studies exist that hint at what may be happening. In 1978 Lawrence Whitehead and I reported that almost 25% of artists who attended two workshops on health issues had a health problem during the preceding year that they thought was related to their work. The most common problems were similar to those seen in industry; namely, rashes and other skin conditions, lung disorders, and back problems.

More recently, a study was made of cause of death listed on the death certificate for all artists famous enough to have an obituary in one or more of several important newspapers. These artists were found to have died from certain types of cancer significantly more often than would be expected for the general public. And the cancers and other diseases that killed them were the types often linked in various studies to occupational exposures to solvents and certain other chemicals.

It is reasonable to assume from the information now available that artists and art students are at greater than average risk of injury and illness because of the types of chemicals and processes to which they are exposed and, because they usually work in environments not designed for safe use of those materials, they are often at greater risk of illness per hour of exposure than are many industrial workers using the same materials. Furthermore, professional artists who put in 50 to 60 or more hours of work a week have a greater number of total hours of exposure than do workers in industry. As a result, it is reasonable to expect that the materials shown to cause problems in industry are causing at least as many—and probably more—problems among artists.

But the fact that materials or processes are potentially hazardous doesn't mean that one has to stop work and close up shop. It is usually possible to keep on working with much less risk through the expenditure of only a relatively small amount of effort and money. The main purpose of this *Guide* is to identify what hazards exist and what risk-reduction methods are most effective and economical. Almost as important a goal, however, is to identify what is NOT hazardous, so that you will not be needlessly anxious or waste effort and money trying to avoid something that is relatively harmless.

II How the Body Interacts with the Environment

Whether a substance or a process presents a problem for few people or for many depends both on the nature of the substance or process and on the ways in which the body and the environment interact. Potentially harmful materials and processes that stress the body (*stressors*) all involve various forms of energy, which have been arbitrarily divided into biological energy and five types of physical energy. These are shown in Table I.

Most chemical and biological stressors get into the body by inhalation or ingestion. What isn't commonly realized, however, is that some of the dust particles that get into the lungs are coughed up and swallowed as phlegm. Thus, they end up not only in the lungs, but in the stomach as well.

A substance inhaled into the lungs may be removed from the air sacs in three ways. If the lungs are in good shape, tiny hairs (or cilia) on the surface cells may sweep the material back out, a process known as clearance. Some fibrous chemicals, such as asbestos, cotton, or silica, have poorly understood characteristics that make them activate defense cells in the lungs. These cells then engulf any of the fibers that haven't been cleared and remove them to the spaces between the air sacs of the lungs. Once there, the fibers get stored for many years. If enough of them collect, these fibers start to reduce breathing efficiency. At first this damage doesn't cause obvious symptoms; but with time, shortness of breath and other symptoms begin to occur. These signs and symptoms constitute a group of storage diseases known as the pneumoconioses. Some of them are well known; silicosis of potters and granite workers, "brown lung" of cotton workers, "black lung" or anthracosis of coal miners, and asbestosis.

The third possibility—most common with gases, fumes, vapors, mists, and the smallest dust particles—is that the inhaled substance is absorbed through the lungs into the blood and gets carried to other parts of the body.

Table 1

Types of stressors, common sources, and modes of entry into body

Stressor Category	Subcategories	Mode of Entry into Body	Typical Material or Process
A. Biological Energy	Bacteria, viruses, fungus, plant or animal allergens	Inhalation, ingestion, invasion of broken skin, rarely (as with allergens) through intact skin	Plant products, animal skins, bone, horn, hair
B. Physical Energy 1. Chemical	Dusts, solvents, gases, vapors, mists, fumes, oils, acids, caustics	Inhalation, ingestion, absorption through broken skin or (rarely) intact skin	All paints, dyes, glazes, inks, solvents, clay, metal, stone, plastics, kiln gases, photographic materials, etc.
2. Kinetic (motion)	Noise, vibration, repetitive or straining motions	Ears, through intact skin, through body motion and muscle tone	Hammers, saws, drills, throwing pots, metalsmithing, lifting or bending activities
3. Thermal	Heat and excessive cold	General or localized exposure to hot or cold environment	Kilns, welding, blacksmithing, processes using cold water
4. Radiation	Ultraviolet and infrared, lasers, microwave, ionizing	Eyes, through intact skin	Ceramic and glass kilns, welding, lasers, radioactive glazes, carbon arcs
5. Electrical		Direct contact with current	Electrically operated machinery and equipment

Chemicals can also get into the bloodstream by ingestion and absorption through the stomach and intestine or, less commonly, by absorption through the skin. The greater the solubility of the chemical, the greater are the chances it will get into the bloodstream.

Some of these chemicals are then excreted through the intestines or the kidneys. Others are broken down or metabolized by key enzyme systems in body organs, usually the liver. Still other chemicals tend to be stored in various locations. This last is especially common with chemicals that are soluble in fats, which tend to be stored in bone marrow, brain and nervous tissue, and other locations where there are large fat accumulations.

Actually, a combination of all three processes goes on, although some chemicals (e.g., lead and other heavy metals) are predominantly stored, others predominantly metabolized (e.g., alcohol), and still others are mostly excreted unchanged. If a very large quantity of chemical is taken into the bloodstream, much of it will be stored for at least a period of time. If only a small amount is taken in, most or all will be immediately metabolized or excreted.

Relatively few chemicals can penetrate unbroken skin. But those solvents that are good degreasing agents can dry out skin by removing body oils; the skin may then crack, develop rashes, or become infected, thus opening the way for chemicals to get through. Some chemicals, such as epoxies, may cause skin allergies by reacting with local tissues instead of passing all the way through the skin. Other chemicals, such as strong acids and bases, or chromate compounds, may eat into skin, causing direct damage to it.

A balance always exists between what comes into the body and what goes out. The amount remaining in the body at any given moment is known as the *body burden*. One key principle in avoiding illness is to keep the body burden for any chemical below the amount that is capable of causing illness for that particular chemical. As I shall discuss shortly, this is done both through methods to reduce intake and through methods to increase breakdown and removal. Another key principle is to use substances that are less toxic; that is, that must be present in very large amounts before they begin to cause illness.

If enough of a stressor remains in the body, its effects will become apparent primarily in the places where quantities of it have been localized. A material stored in fatty tissue will cause disorders of bone, blood formation, and nervous tissue. One mostly excreted through the kidneys will cause kidney and bladder disease. Materials excreted through the intestine or metabolized by the liver will act by causing gastrointestinal symptoms.

The skin, as the largest organ in the body, will have contact with excessive amounts of many harmful materials that may cause rashes, infections, or other forms of dermatitis. Excessive strain from repetitive movement of or vibration to the hands and wrists may show up as localized disorders, such as white fingers or carpal tunnel syndrome, while similar stresses to the back result in potter's or weaver's back and other aptly named painful back disabilities.

It is important to realize, however, that some diseases, especially cancers and the pneumoconioses, may not become apparent until after a latent or quiescent period of 10–30 years of exposure. By the time they do become apparent, the damage to the body is often too extensive to permit one to recapture function already lost.

What are the factors that increase the likelihood of illness? These can be divided into two categories: factors that increase the body burden, and factors that increase the chances that a person will become sick at a given body burden. These are listed below.

A. Factors that may increase body burden:
    1. Using large amounts of a material, or using smaller but still excessive amounts very often
    2. Storing materials in uncovered containers
    3. Being exposed to similar chemicals when not doing art. The artist exposed to asbestos or lead at work is also exposed to these materials on city streets from asbestos in brake linings and lead in gasoline
    4. Working in a small, poorly ventilated space
    5. Having a dirty studio
    6. Wearing studio clothes when not working in studio
    7. Failing to use protective clothing or equipment
    8. Smoking cigarettes or marihuana (picks up materials on the cigarette, and also reduces lung clearance)
    9. Consuming alcohol during work or lunch break (acts as a solvent to some chemicals entering the body and competes with enzyme systems that destroy other chemicals)
    10. Working long hours
    11. (For vibration) Absent or improper damping of equipment that can vibrate

B. Factors that increase chances of illness at a given body burden
    1. Cigarette smoking (interacts with asbestos and other chemicals to cause cancer and lung disease)
    2. Heavy drinking (5 or more drinks at a sitting; intensifies the damage caused to liver by other chemicals)
    3. History of allergies
    4. Chronic diseases, such as previous heart, lung, kidney or liver diseases, seizures
    5. Use of toxic chemicals when less toxic ones would do
    6. Pregnancy (increased risk is primarily to the fetus)
    7. Extreme youth (rapidly growing tissues are often more sensitive to toxic effects)

Finally, mention should be made of the range of response within a population, which is known as the *biological gradient of disease*. Of a group of people minimally exposed to a moderately hazardous substance, a few will get very sick, while most will not get sick or will get only mildly ill. But as the exposure increases, the latter will get sick or severely ill. A few individuals at the other end of the spectrum may show little or no effects despite receiving massive doses.

Those individuals who are uniquely sensitive usually find that out rather soon. This *Guide* is not aimed at them but at the remainder of the population. Unfortunately, because of the latency phenomenon described earlier, the people who think they are especially hardy may not learn otherwise until it is too late to undertake preventive measures. The *Guide*, therefore, is also for those who think they are of the hardy breed.

III What You Need To Know about Dusts and Solvents

Special attention is being given to the health hazards of dusts and solvents because these materials are ubiquitous in the artist's studio. Dust is created during manipulation of many solid materials, and moist or even liquid materials may become dust if they are not cleaned up but allowed to dry. Solvents are the primary method by which most art materials are put into workable form. The only common materials not requiring solvents for the forming process are stone, heating of glass and metals, and manipulation of fibers, wood, leather, and bone. If you understand general characteristics of these two classes of materials you can often protect yourself even if you don't know the specific material or its characteristics. *This general information, however, is not meant as a substitute for more specific information, if you can get it.*

Dust
Any material that can become dust should be treated as a potential source of dust. This includes wet clay and glazes, and wet paints, inks, etc.

Very large dust particles are unlikely to get into the body through inhalation because they are too heavy to be carried far in the air. Somewhat smaller particles get into the mouth, nose, and throat, where they cause irritation, and may then be coughed up as phlegm and swallowed, thus getting into the body through ingestion.

The particles most likely to get into the lungs are those smaller than 10 microns in size, or just smaller than the tiniest particles that can be seen floating in a brightly lit room or in the beam of light from a slide projector. These particles present a problem because they are light enough to keep floating at nose and mouth level for several hours after they get stirred up. Once they are breathed in, they are also light enough to get carried into the lungs. There they are small enough to be either completely swallowed by defensive cells and stored or (if smaller than 1 micron) absorbed through the lungs into the bloodstream.

Depending on their particular chemical characteristics, some dust particles may cause storage disease, others lung allergies and cancers, while those that get into the bloodstream may cause toxicity or poisoning. Some flammable materials become explosive when in dust form simply by floating in the room.

Many people wonder how much dust is harmful. Unfortunately, many chemicals are sufficiently toxic so that breathing in an amount of dust smaller than the size of the nose or ear on a Roosevelt dime per cubic meter of air (about a cubic yard in size) can be hazardous if it is done regularly over an eight-hour day. And a similar pinch *in toto* may be harmful if ingested into the stomach.

The keys to control of dust are:

1. Try to create as little dust as possible by keeping materials in moist state and by storing them in closed containers.

2. Each day clean up any dust created. This is especially important in classrooms, where scheduled clean-up assignments may have to be given out and enforced for students. *Do cleanup at the end of the work day* so that any fine dust raised is in the breathing zone at a time when there is no one there to breathe it. *Never clean up just before starting to work.*

3. Always use a wet process for cleaning, such as damp cloths or damp mopping, or use of damp sweeping compounds, liberally applied. *Never dry sweep!* Dry vacuuming creates dust, and should never be attempted unless one has a specialized, extremely expensive (more than $500) machine designed specifically to remove and trap almost all particles down to smaller than a half micron. Wet vacuums are usually not very effective, because they spit out a lot of the dust through the discharge end. They should be used only if trapping filters for toxic or other specific dusts have been attached to the discharge.

4. Use an appropriate ventilation system for all dusty procedures. This is described in the next chapter. The above comments apply as well to mists, fumes, and similar aerosols, which also tend to float for long hours at the level of the breathing zone and which may dry up and form dust as they float.

Solvents

A wide variety of liquids function as solvents for the artist. By far the most common solvent—but usually not recognized as such—is water. Therefore, occasional statements that all solvents are harmful, or that pregnant women should avoid all solvents, are not entirely accurate. Some of the more common solvents, together with some examples and their key characteristics, are listed in Table II.

As a general rule, and unless you know otherwise, treat all organic solvents (items 2–7 in the Table) as if they

1. can cause both acute and chronic damage to the nervous system,

2. can damage the liver,

3. can degrease the skin if not properly handled, and

4. are flammable. (It is important to know, however, that most solvents are a health hazard at concentrations lower than those at which they are a safety hazard.)

Treat acids and bases (item 8 in the Table) as if they can severely damage skin and irritate lungs and eyes.

The rules for working with solvents are:

1. Store them in covered and preferably nonbreakable containers.

2. Use them only in the presence of adequate localized ventilation (see next chapter).

3. Keep open only the smallest amount necessary for the work at hand, and replace that from the closed storage as it gets used up.

4. Try to substitute safer solvents for less safe ones, whenever possible. Table III lists some typical solvents according to their relative safety. In cleaning up a silk screen, for example, you might wish to use larger quantities of a safer material for the initial cleanup, and then finish the final cleanup with a small quantity of a more toxic but stronger solvent.

5. Be sure to place all dirty rags, paper towels, etc., containing inks and other solvents in closed storage, since solvents in these can also seep into the air. So can solvents that paint brushes are sitting in. They should be kept covered as well.

6. Use flammable (i.e., have flash points at temperatures less than 100°F) or explosive solvents in a flame-free and spark-free environment, and have an adequate size ABC rated fire extinguisher available.

7. Apply a hand lotion twice a day to replace oils in the skin that have been removed, even if the solvent you are using is water.

Table II

Categories of Solvents and Their Characteristics

Category of Solvent	Examples	Important Characteristics
1. Water	Solvent for clay, most glazes, water colors, dyes	Causes cracking of skin with excessive immersion, nontoxic, nonflammable
2. Straight chain (aliphatic) hydrocarbons	Gasoline, kerosene, turpentine, mineral spirits	Flammable, may be heavier than air, central nervous system (CNS) depressants, can damage nervous tissue, liver, kidneys, eyes, lungs. Degrease skin.
3. Ring (Aromatic) hydrocarbons	Benzene and benzene derivatives, toluene, Xylene	Flammable, CNS and bone marrow depressants, can damage liver, lungs, sometimes cause cancer. Degrease skin.
4. Halogenated hydrocarbons (both aromatic and aliphatic)	Chloroform, carbon tetrachloride, perchlorethylene	Usually nonflammable, severe CNS depression and liver damage. Degrease skin.
5. Alcohols	Methyl (wood) and ethyl alcohol, glycerin	CNS depression and damage, liver damage. Degrease skin.
6. Aldehydes, ketones, esters	Formaldehyde, acetone, methyl ethyl ketone (MEK), ethyl acetate	Flammable; affect skin, lungs, kidneys.
7. Ethers	Glycol ethers or cellosolves	CNS depression, liver damage, explosive. Degrease skin. Possible damage to fetus.
8. Acids & Bases	Nitric, sulfuric, hydrochloric acid, lye, vinegar	Soluble in water. May heat up and splash on mixing concentrated solution with water, cause severe burns of skin, eyes, lungs on even brief direct contact or inhalation.

Table III
Relative Toxicity and Flammability of Some Solvents

To Be Avoided Completely, If Possible
> Benzene or Benzol* (Benzine is OK)**
> Carbon Tetrachloride**
> Chloroform**
> Trichlorethylene**
> Methyl Butyl Ketone (MBK)*
> Methyl Cellosolve Acetate**
> Possibly Hexane (Recent data suggest excessive toxicity in rubber-cement users)

Highly Toxic on Inhalation
   Alcohols and Aromatic Hydrocarbons
> Isoamyl alcohol (Fusel oil)
> Toluene* and **
> Xylene* and **
> Styrene*
> Vinyl Toluene
> α Methyl Styrene

   Ketones and Cellosolves
> Isophorone
> Cyclohexanone
> Methyl Cellosolve**
> Butyl Cellosolve**

   *Chlorinated Hydrocarbons***
> Ethylene Dichloride
> Methylene Chloride (Forms Carbon Monoxide)
> I.I.I. Trichlroethane (Methyl Chloroform)
> Perchlorethylene
> Ortho-Dichlorobenzene
> Monochlorotoluene

Most chlorinated hydrocarbons are not flammable but form poisonous phosgene gas in presence of flame, ultraviolet light, or high heat.

Some Less Hazardous Solvents on Inhalation
> Lithotine (Good Choice)
> Turpentine* and **
> Cutting Oils
> Cyclohexane*
> Kerosene
> Mineral Spirits (Good Choice)
> VM & P Naptha (Benzine)*
> Rubber Solvent*
> Gasoline* and **
> Cellosolve**
> Cellosolve Acetate**
> Ethylene Glycol**
> Diethylene Glycol**
> Carbitol**
> Methyl Isobutyl Ketone (MIBK, Hexone)*
> Methyl Ethyl Ketone (MEK)*
> Acetone* (Good Choice)
> Isoamyl Acetate (Banana Oil)*
> Butyl Acetate*
> Ethyl Acetate*
> Methyl Chloroform (Good Choice for Chlorinated Hydrocarbon)
> Benzyl Alcohol (Good Choice)
> Ethyl Alcohol*
> Isopropyl Alcohol*
> Butyl Alcohol*
> Methyl Alcohol (Wood Alcohol)* and **

*Flammable.

**Some absorption through skin.

Some data suggest that cellosolves may be associated with birth defects when used by either sex.

Those solvents designated good choice have been so labeled based only on their relative toxicity. They may or may not meet your particular needs, but are worth a try if you are currently using more toxic materials and cannot obtain adequate ventilation.

8. Always add the chemical to the water when mixing concentrated acids or bases with water. Never add the water to the chemical, since it might cause small drops of water to boil, splash up and burn you.

9. Always wear protective goggles and gloves when working with concentrated acids or bases.

10. Immediately wash off any acid or base—even if not concentrated—that gets on your skin with large amounts of running water. Keep washing for at least 10–15 minutes. If your skin feels at all "soapy" or irritated, continue washing. If more than a small area is burned see a physician.

11. Have materials on hand for rapid cleanup of spills. Some safety-supply houses sell special clean-up materials for rapid absorption of chemical spills. A good supply of kitty litter or vermiculite can be helpful.

IV A General Approach to Studio Safety

This chapter considers first the least expensive approaches and then the more expensive ones. Usually, however, the expenses are within the means of the many artists who have very little money.

Smoking

If you are a smoker, stopping smoking is probably the best single thing you can do to protect your health as an artist. Cigarette smoking not only is harmful by itself but also interacts with a number of art materials and processes to make *them* more hazardous.

Clean up

Proper clean-up techniques yield very high safety return for the time spent. Clean up every day at the end of the work period. Use moist cleaning techniques, instead of dry sweeping or vacuuming. Easily wiped cloth, linoleum, stone, glass, or plastic work surfaces are helpful. Newspaper or other disposable materials placed under the work can sometimes speed cleanup. If you are cleaning up solvents or materials that evaporate easily *do not* leave the rags or kitty litter in an open container. Place them either in a covered container or, better yet, outside the building.

Storage

Mention has been made of covered storage as a method for reducing escape of dust and of solvents and liquids that can evaporate easily. Try to store large quantities of these materials away from active work or walk areas. Cover bags of clay and similar materials with plastic so that spillage will be contained should the bags break open. Flammable material should be kept in flame-resistant containers (which, unfortunately, are expensive). Sources for these and other safety equipment are listed in the appendix.

Some materials, such as dyestuffs and mordants, are repackaged by suppliers from large drums and are shipped in unmarked or poorly marked paper or plastic bags. These should be repackaged in more durable containers and should have the label clear taped to the container so that the tape completely covers the label and keeps it clean. Better yet, notify your supplier that you would appreciate better packaging and clearer labeling for purposes of health and safety.

Timing of Activities

If you must use a fairly toxic material for which you can't find a less toxic substitute, try to time your activities so that you allow two or three week rest breaks between the occasions when you use it. In this way, any of the chemical that gets taken into your body has time to be removed or metabolized by the body before you add another insult. Thus, you can use time as a method for reducing body burden. Similarly, any activities that strain back or wrist muscles, or cause noise or vibration, should be done for only short periods of time (e.g., half-hour stretches) and alternated with another activity for a similar time span. This also gives the body a chance to recover.

Avoiding Back Problems

Avoid back problems by getting comfortable seating with good light, getting up and walking around or changing position periodically, and having a set of preventive exercises that you perform at least three times a week. No single group of exercises is *the* answer. Choose one exercise that will stretch back muscles by forcing you to lean way back or to stretch towards the ceiling. Another exercise should be aimed at strengthening abdominal muscles (e.g., sit ups), since these muscles play a very important, but often underestimated, role in supporting the back. A third group of rotational exercises should be carried out to put your back and shoulders through their entire range of motion, thus giving you full flexibility.

Hand Care

Use a hand lotion at least twice a day to keep skin from cracking. If you are engaged in a procedure that might be damaged by grease or wax resist, put the lotion on just after washing up for lunch and dinner rather than before beginning to work.

Eating

Never eat in the work area. Apart from cigarette smoking, there is no better way for getting toxic materials into your mouth than eating in the studio. Always wash your hands before taking a meal.

Noise & Vibration

Noise and vibration can sometimes be reduced by using felt, rubber, sponge, rug, or other damping materials under equipment. Such materials are often available either as scrap or at low cost.

Protective Clothing and Equipment

Safety goggles cost from $2–$5 and are highly recommended. Try to get a goggle with covered sides so that flying particles or caustic liquids can't get in from the sides. Eye injuries have been a relatively common problem among my artist friends who were not wearing goggles or were wearing inadequate ones. If hot particles or caustic liquids are flying about, you may wish to have a full face mask. These cost $15–$20.

All activities requiring observation of hot flame (looking in kilns, glass blowing, welding, cutting, and brazing) should be done with welding goggles. Use the darkest filter you can see with to prevent the occurrence of cataracts. These cost about $10. Cataract surgery costs about $2000. If you use goggles and you still see occasional white spots before your eyes, switch to a darker shade or filter. Goggles to fit every need, from grinding operations to laser beam use, are available from safety-equipment suppliers. They are designed for specific use, so they are not interchangeable from one work process to another.

Special goggles are designed for use with (1) Noncorrosive dust: These goggles have heat-treated or filter lenses with wide-screen ventilators around the eyecup for air circulation; (2) Welding: OSHA regulation 29 CRF 1910.252 (e) provides a guide for selecting the proper lenses to fit each welding job; (3) Stone and wood: Chippers' goggles have contoured rigid plastic eyecups and are designed to be worn with or without eyeglasses; and (4) Lasers: These goggles are designed for use with specific wave lengths of laser radiation and should not be used for different wave lengths. Information on exposure criteria for lasers, as well as technical details regarding uses and hazards, is available in the National Safety Council bulletins *Accident Prevention Manual for Industrial Operations* and *Fundamentals of Industrial Hygiene*.

Goggles used by more than one person should be taken apart, washed in soap and warm water, and immersed in a disinfectant solution after each use. Such solutions are available from goggle suppliers.

For those who wear glasses or contact lenses there are special problems. Since the NSC *Fundamentals of Industrial Hygiene* reports that liquids and dusts can penetrate behind the lenses, an appropriate pair of goggles worn over glasses or contact lenses offers greater protection. Some recent studies have shown that where chemical splashes are possible, contact lenses help to protect the eyes, but some welding manuals say contact lenses can be dangerous. General agreement exists that contact lenses alone do not provide reliable eye protection.

Sustained noise levels above 90 decibels (db) eventually cause deafness. If you have to talk at much above your usual speaking voice in order to be heard, or if you have occasional ringing in your ears after working in your studio, you are exceeding the 90db threshold. Try first the damping methods described above. If these do not reduce the noise level enough, use ear protectors whenever the noisy processes are in operation. These range in cost from about $2 for small ear plugs to as much as $20 for deluxe model earmuffs. The noise that is blocked out is the excess amount above 90 db; so you can still hear what is going on around you.

Reserve a set of clothing for wearing exclusively in the studio. Work clothes should include an apron or coveralls and a hat or kerchief to keep dust and other material out of your hair. If possible, wash work clothes separately from your other laundry to avoid contaminating your pillows, towels, and everyday clothing. If you are exposed to hot or caustic processes, you may wish to invest in aprons, sleeves, or gauntlets made of special protective materials. Vinyl aprons sell for less than $5, rubber ones for about $10, and the heat resistant variety for about $40. Vinyl sleeve protectors are about $4 a pair. Heat resistant sleeves of kevlar are twice as expensive.

For heavy work involving large sculpture, etc., hard hats are recommended. These begin at about $4–$5. Steel capped shoes, which are more expensive, are also recommended.

If you are using flammable processes or materials you need an adequate size ABC fire extinguisher.

Masks Versus Ventilation

Protection from toxic chemicals is much more effectively provided by an adequate ventilation system than by the wearing of a mask. A mask is cumbersome, uncomfortable, inefficient, and inadequate for most hazardous activities. The specific reasons that masks are not recommended follow:

1. They are unsuitable for men with beards. There is enough leakage around the beard so that even the best fitting mask cannot filter out very much.
2. They are so uncomfortable after about 15 minutes of wear that most people tend not to wear them regularly or continuously.
3. They are useful only for filtering out low levels of exposure.
4. They must be worn not only by the artist carrying out the hazardous procedure but also by everyone present in the studio, if the concentration of the contaminant is high. And they must be worn for some time after the procedure is ended in order to give the toxic substance time to dissipate or settle out.
5. They require different filters for different types of chemicals, and each filter costs additional money.
6. They need frequent cleaning, storage in an uncontaminated container, and frequent change of filters (as often as every two weeks).

Nevertheless, masks have a useful, if limited, place in the art studio. If you have a specific procedure that is engaged in no more often than two or three times a week, to which only one or two people will be exposed, and that will last less than a half hour in a relatively isolated area of the studio, it may be worthwhile to use a mask—that is, provided you don't have a beard. Mixing clay is a good example of such an activity. Daily 5–10 minute wet sweeping of the floor is another appropriate time to wear a dust mask. But, for any sustained hazardous activity, masks are not appropriate.

In choosing a mask the first consideration is to get one that will filter out the types of substances you will be exposed to. Masks for filtration of room air are basically of two types. One has a single type-fixed filter, and the entire mask usually gets thrown out, or (less commonly) the filter gets replaced, when it has become clogged. This type of mask is useful for water-based paint and nuisance dusts (e.g., wood, plaster, house dust). *Only if it has a NIOSH label saying it is suitable for "toxic dusts,"* can it be used also for toxic dusts such as silica, asbestos, cotton, and other dusts that cause pneumonconiosis. The fixed filter mask usually sells for less than $5.

The second type of mask is the cartridge type with replaceable filters. These are more expensive ($15–$25 for the mask plus about $6 for each type of filter; if more than one filter type is needed, the cost then goes up by increments of $6) but more versatile than the fixed filter mask, because one can change types of filters, or sometimes use two different filters at one time, in order to be protected against various materials. Filters are made for such substances as fumes, toxic dusts, asbestos, organic vapors, acid mists, ammonia, chlorine, and some radioactive materials. It is essential to choose a mask that is specific to the material you are using. Simply going into a paint or hardware store or any army surplus store to "pick up" a mask is throwing out money.

The next issue is to choose a mask that fits your face. Some manufacturers now make masks in small, medium, and large sizes. The mask should have two straps, one each for the top and bottom of the mask, and it should feel comfortable with both straps on, but you should feel no air coming from anywhere other than through the cartridges. If you block off the mask intake, you should feel as if you are unable to breathe.

After using the mask, clean the inside and outside with a damp cloth, let it dry, and place it in a plastic bag for storage. If you leave a mask sitting around uncovered and face up when it is not in use, you are simply creating a receptacle to gather all floating dust and other material, which you will then breathe in as soon as you put the mask on.

With time the filters get clogged. You can tell that this is happening because it gets increasingly difficult to breathe through the mask. When this occurs, replace the filter. Replace cartridges for gases if odor is apparent when wearing the mask.

An effective ventilation system that can serve multiple functions is a more sensible investment of money and effort than are masks. With some personal labor and ingenuity, one may get a perfectly adequate ventilation system for as little as $25–$50. Probably $75–$100 is a more reasonable expectation, although for a large studio with very dusty, toxic, or flammable procedures it is possible to spend considerably more, especially if you do none of the labor yourself.

The subject of ventilation engineering is so complex that specialized engineering degrees are given in this subject. The appendix lists an excellent reference that is considered the standard text for those who are not ventilation engineers. But it is possible to design and build a quite adequate system simply by following the principles and guidelines below.

There are three types of ventilation. The first is called *passive ventilation,* such as opening a window and hoping that enough hazardous material will diffuse out or be sucked out if it is a windy day. This method can never be relied on. It is not an adequate ventilation system.

The second method is called *general* or *dilution ventilation.* Fresh air is introduced into a room, usually near floor level, and "old" air is removed through a fan or duct near the ceiling. This method clears out or changes *all* the air in a room periodically, anywhere from 5–6 times per hour for an average room to three times that often for a lavatory. General ventilation is for purposes of comfort only. Although it is not much more effective than passive ventilation in protecting health and safety, it is the most common type of ventilation in school buildings and other public places. It is also, unfortunately, the only method many architects and contractors consider when designing home studios.

The third and only useful type of ventilation for the artist is *active localized ventilation*. "Active" refers to the use of a fan that will actively move air with its contaminants. "Localized" refers to the fact that the only air to be moved is that immediately surrounding the source of the contamination; e.g., a clay mixer, a spray painting or glazing process, a plastic sculpture that is hardening, or a series of lithographs or paintings that are drying by releasing their solvent into the air. Incidentally, by removing only the contaminated air in the localized area, this type of ventilation saves considerable heating costs in winter because it evacuates only the heated air that is most hazardous, and leaves the rest of the heated air in the studio.

There are several basic requirements for establishing active localized ventilation. The contaminant source must be enclosed as much as possible. The fan must generate enough velocity to remove most or all of the contaminated air and to keep the concentration of the contaminant below a toxic level. In the process of the removal, however, the contaminant must not be moved past the breathing area of the person who is doing the work. Finally, the contaminated air that is removed must not be dumped in a location where it will endanger other individuals. I shall consider each of these steps, as well as a few related issues necessary to understand and provide proper ventilation design and operation.

Enclosing the Contaminant Source

Ideally, the work you are doing should be enclosed on top, back, and two sides, with just enough space for you to work comfortably. Some jewelers have cut open large metal cans (e.g., a 20-lb. honey tin) and inserted a duct in the top or back. One can also make a hood-type enclosure out of wood, metal, plastic, or other material. A typical hood might have a 2- by 2-foot opening in front. This enclosure can be placed permanently in a single location, or it can be made portable with flexible ducting (e.g., clothes-dryer type) so that it can be moved from one location to another. If two or more procedures require ventilation, try to carry them out at locations as close together as possible.

If you are working with a larger operation, especially of a temporary nature, you may be able to enclose the entire area with a shower curtain, plastic film, or similar sort of material that will limit the area to be ventilated to several cubic feet. Sometimes it is not at all possible to surround the process. In that case, you need to pay particular attention to getting the fan, or ventilation duct leading to the fan, as close to the work as possible—2 to 3 inches away is not too close; and if you don't have a very powerful fan, 12 inches may be too far. Again, flexible ducting permits you to move the duct very close to your work as the work itself gets moved about.

Ensuring Adequate Velocity

Start by considering the fan size. The rule of thumb is that each square foot of enclosure opening requires a net fan capability to move 100 cubic feet of air per minute (cfm) for gases or 200 cfm for dusts or mists. Thus, the 2- by 2-foot opening noted above equals 4 square feet and requires a net fan capability of 400–800 cfm. Several factors, however, reduce the efficiency of a fan, so the actual fan size needed is likely to be considerably larger than 400–800 cfm.

If the contaminant source is not completely enclosed, efficiency is markedly reduced. Very narrow and long ducting also decreases efficiency. If possible, try to arrange your work so that it will need no more than 4–5 feet of ducting before discharge to the outside, and use ducting that has few curves, or gentle ones, and is 6 inches or larger in diameter. Again, the duct opening should be as close to the work as possible. A fan sucking air loses 90% of its efficiency by the time one has moved one duct diameter (6 inches!) away from the end of the duct. As you can see, even with a duct quite close to the work, one would probably want to get a fan rated at least for 800–1200 cfm in order to ensure a net flow of 400 cfm.

The efficiency of a fan can be increased by taking the contaminant in the direction it ordinarily wants to go. Hot gases and fumes seek to rise; therefore, don't try to draw them downward. Dusts tend to settle; therefore, don't try to pull them upward.

The overall system can be tested by placing a smoky candle where your work would be, turning on the system, and watching to see if the smoke is pulled strongly in the direction of the duct. If this does not happen, several corrective measures are possible: better enclosure, a shorter duct of larger diameter, removal of kinks and nonstreamlined areas in the duct that might cause eddy currents, and, if nothing else works, a larger fan. A small fan behind you blowing in the direction of the sucking fan can also improve efficiency, since a blowing fan, before it gets down to 10% efficiency, can function at 15 times the distance of a sucking fan.

Avoiding Sucking Contaminants into Your Breathing Area

Arrange the fan or duct so that contaminated air is pulled to the side, back, or downward, rather than up past your nose. Contaminated air should never be pulled so that it goes up past your nose towards the wall or ceiling or comes from in front of you to behind you. All procedures for air removal must include provision for addition of fresh make-up air (through a slightly open door, window, or vent from another room). Otherwise, a vacuum, which would prevent you from opening the door to the studio, might be created. Fresh intake air should be coming in from behind you.

Avoiding Contamination of Others

Find out where contaminated air will discharge from your studio. It should vent outside the building, where it will not be distributed to other rooms. If prevailing winds at the point of discharge will carry the contaminated air past other windows or across your vegetable garden, add enough outside ducting to move the air beyond these locations.

Other Important Ventilation Issues

It is desirable in some cases, such as those involving mixtures of fine and heavy dust, to have the duct go through a barrel, bag, or other removable receptable so that the heavier dust can drop out and be collected. The efficiency of the fan in removing finer dust is thereby improved.

When dealing with flammable or explosive materials, it is necessary to use a special fan system that does not create sparks. Such a system is, unfortunately, quite expensive, but essential for fire safety.

Fan blades and ducts should be cleaned periodically. If dusty procedures are involved, consider getting a centrifugal (or squirred-cage) fan with a radial blade, since this type of blade positioning tends to promote self-cleaning during operation.

What do you do if you are in a location without windows, and it is not possible to make a hole in a wall? An article in *Ceramics Monthly* (April 1983) describes how to make a portable system using a wet-dry vacuum fitted with discharge filters. This should be adequate for intermittent operation, provided the filters are changed periodically.

If a more powerful fan is needed, you may find it necessary to weigh the ability to ventilate enough air against the amount of noise that such a fan might create. Fans with larger diameter blades can move more air while turning at slow speed than can smaller fans at slow speed. If you need greater power, therefore, but are worried about the amount of noise, consider getting a fan with bigger blades, rather than a smaller one that rotates faster. Also, check on adequate, well-damped suspension straps for ducting to reduce unnecessary vibration that translates into noise.

Fire Protection

Many materials, particularly solvents, are flammable. Moreover, some dusts are explosive, and certain solvents form highly toxic gases in the presence of flame or heat. Therefore, such materials, and rags used for cleanup, must be stored in special fire safety containers. Ventilation for such materials must use spark-free motors and equipment. For the latter, professional advice should be sought.

Particular attention should be given to fire extinguishers. Type A extinguishers are useful only for flammable wood, paper, and similar material, but not for flammable liquids, which require a type B extinguisher, or for electrical fires, which require a type C extinguisher. It is best to get combination ABC extinguishers. As a minimum, get a UL-listed size 2A 10BC, or even larger, that can be refilled.

If you are using flammable metals you need a type D extinguishing material. This does not come in an extinguisher but in a container from which you scoop the material onto the fire. The flammable metals are magnesium, lithium, titanium, zinc, calcium, sodium, and potassium.

Read the instructions on the extinguisher *before* a fire occurs. Check periodically to be sure the extinguisher still is the proper weight or has the indicator needle in the green charge zone. Some simple rules for using a fire extinguisher follow:
1. If fire occurs, *first* be sure everyone around has been alerted and gets out.
2. *Second,* call the fire department.
3. Only then consider if the fire is still small enough to put it out yourself. If not, get out immediately. If yes, be sure *you* have an escape route.
4. Pull the release pin on the fire extinguisher. Hold it *upright*. With an ABC extinguisher you have a charge that will last only 15–20 seconds! *Stand no closer than 6–10 feet away.* Aim at the *base* of the fire beginning *nearest you* and press the handle, *sweeping back and forth* across the fire at its base or source. Continue sweeping back and forth even after it has gone out.
5. If you are using an ABC extinguisher some of the powder will cover everything and may even kick back at you. Work carefully so that you don't blow the flammable materials around.
6. Once the fire is out, get out immediately so you don't get trapped if it suddenly flares up again.
7. Soon after the fire, take the extinguisher to a supplier to be recharged.

V The Special Needs of Children and Pregnant Women

When working with children it is necessary to keep in mind their greater sensitivity to small amounts of hazardous materials, their inexperience, and their lesser manipulative skills that make them likely to spill or splash materials. Only the first of these issues is important in protecting the fetus of a pregnant woman.

1. If pregnant or when working with children under age 10–12, try to use less toxic substitutes for more toxic materials. In particular, water-based materials are far preferable to those requiring organic solvents. Choose materials designated by the Art and Craft Materials Institute (see appendix) as appropriate for children.

2. Do not use any aerosols with children or if you are pregnant.

3. If clay, glazes, dyes, or other materials that require mixing or preparation are used, do such preparation before children arrive (and, if possible, do cleanup after they leave) to limit their exposure.

4. Measure out only as much material as the children are likely to need in the time available. This limits possibilities of large spills or of contamination from open containers.

5. Be sure everyone is wearing a protective apron or other protection over regular clothing.

6. Prepare sufficient cleanup materials in advance to avoid a delay in cleanup if any spills do occur.

7. Demonstrate proper handwashing techniques to children and supervise closely their clean-up process. Never let children leave the studio without washing their hands. If you don't have washing facilities, you shouldn't be using potentially hazardous art materials!

You may not be feeling ill while engaged in a process creating dust, vapors, fumes, or mist. But if others around you, especially children, are complaining of the odor, or headaches, or similar discomforts it is a sure sign that the concentration of the material is too great for health and safety.

VI Dealing with Physicians

Most physicians have little or no training in occupational medicine. Often, they do not recognize the signs and symptoms caused by the hazardous materials to which their artist patients are exposed and confuse them with similar signs and symptoms associated with other, more common medical problems. For this reason, the artist must make his or her profession, his or her activities, and the contaminants to which he or she has been exposed very clear to the physician. *Your regular physician needs to know that you are an artist and what you working with or doing.*

You can assist the physician in making a diagnosis by keeping an occupational-exposure diary listing each of the chemicals or materials you are using by trade name (if that is all you know) or by specific ingredients (if you can determine those) and the frequency of exposure (one time only, intermittent, frequent, or constant.) In the past, manufacturers and suppliers have usually not listed ingredients. Under a new voluntary standard (ASTMD 4236) some labeling of hazardous ingredients may start showing up in the near future. If the material is not labeled you can request that the manufacturer send a "Material Safety Data Sheet," which they are required by law to have; or you may be able to get information about contents from sources listed in the appendix.

You should also know the following:
1. How to determine if a particular bout of ill health may be related to your work. Be suspicious if:
    a) You develop asthma as an adult. Asthma in children has a variety of causes. Asthma beginning in an adult almost invariably is from an environmental contaminant.
    b) Your symptoms are worse when you work (especialy after long sessions) and get better when you stop or stay away from work.
    c) You begin to have an increase in the frequency or severity of respiratory infections, especially of the chest, or start getting short of breath.
    d) You are having rashes or skin problems.
    e) You are getting frequent dizzy spells, areas of numbness, tingling, or other altered sensation, especially if you are working with organic solvents, or you are doing a repetitive hand process and your fingers start getting numb.
    f) You have ringing in your ears and are involved in a noisy operation.

2. What routine preventive tests you need periodically.

   a) If you are exposed to dusts, or to solvents that may affect lung function, you should get a pulmonary function test every two or three years. This involves blowing as hard and as fast as you can into a tube attached to a metering device, which measures the total amount of air your lungs can hold and how rapidly they can expand. This ability varies according to your age, sex, and body size, and, even if you are in good health, it decreases at a standard rate as you get older. The first test tells how you compare with the standard for your age and sex, and gives you a personal baseline for comparison with subsequent tests, which then measure whether the decrease is in the expected range or is occurring more rapidly than expected and, therefore, suggests problems.
   This technique identifies early lung disease about 8–10 years sooner than does an X-ray, and does not expose you to radiation. It is not a routine test for healthy people under about age 40–50 unless they are involved in dusty trades or other hazardous occupation. Some physicians who are not aware that artists are exposed to these hazards have tried to talk their patients out of having it done. Your response should be that you have been exposed to materials similar to those that cause silicosis (or granite worker's disease) and that you feel it is important.

   b) If exposed to noise, you should have a hearing test done every 2–3 years.

   c) Unless you are feeling ill, however, you usually do not need routine tests for heavy metals unless you are working with materials containing lead. Tests for heavy metals are expensive and difficult to perform and interpret. The sample has to be collected in special glassware that has had all heavy metal contaminants removed.

3. How to communicate with your physician if you think your health problem is related to your work.

As already suggested, adequate consideration of possible work-related illness depends largely on your informing the physician that you are an artist working with potentially hazardous materials in the amounts and at the frequencies listed in your occupational-exposure diary.

Physicians who know little about occupational medicine may initially respond to your medical complaint by suggesting that there is no relationship between your health status and your work. That, of course, may be correct. Or, if a relationship is found, he or she may urge you to stop your work. Although that may also be correct, other options may exist of which the physician not knowledgeable in occupational medicine may not be aware.

Do not be afraid, therefore, to ask for a second opinion. Three or four of the medical specialties have frequent enough contacts with environmentally related illnesses so that their practitioners are less likely to miss important diagnostic clues or to offer "off the wall" solutions.

There are specialists in occupational medicine, but their number is small, and practitioners are not always available. The appendix indicates how you can find out where such help may be obtained near where you live. Also quite knowledgeable concerning environmental problems involving their particular specialty areas are allergists, dermatologists, and specialists in pulmonary or lung diseases. Among the remaining specialties some—but not all—neurologists are alert to environmental causes of disease.

Removing oneself entirely from hazardous material or process is sometimes necessary, especially for individuals with extreme allergic sensitivities. But, it is often possible instead to use better ventilation, improved housekeeping procedures, timing of work to reduce frequency of exposure and permit the body to purge itself, protective clothing, substitution of other, less-hazardous materials that give similar aesthetic results, or the other preventive steps that have already been discussed. These steps obviously cannot prevent illness that has already occurred, but they can give the body a chance to mobilize its own healing processes to the extent that the effects are not irreversible and to prevent further damage.

Studio Guides to Specific Mediums

The following guides provide information about specific aspects of various mediums that require application of the general principles and protective methods described in the first section.

1. Ceramics

	Type of Exposure	Nature of Problem
Chemical	Clay bodies	Most contain free silica, which can cause silicosis of lungs.
	Talcs	Most contain asbestos, which can cause lung disease or, rarely, cancers.
	Asbestos gloves	See above. All asbestos products yield free fibers.
	Glazes, stains, and clay additives, such as barium compounds	Vary widely in toxicity, but all glazes are capable of some degree of chronic poisoning. Chromium, lithium, and nickel compounds can irritate and ulcerate skin.
	Kiln gases	Contain sulfur dioxide, carbon monoxide, and other decomposition pollutants, as well as glaze components.
	Salt glazes	Release chlorine gas, which combines with moisture in air to form hydrochloric acid, which causes acute lung and eye damage.
	Fiber glass and mineral wool	Acute irritation of eyes, skin, and lungs. No known chronic effects have yet been found.
	Plaster of Paris	Nuisance dust only.
Kinetic	Repetitive back strain, especially from throwing.	Potter's back
	Repetitive trauma to wrist from throwing, wedging, etc.	Carpal tunnel syndrome (nerve inflammation)

	Type of Exposure	Nature of Problem
Radiation	Looking in kiln	Cataracts
	Uranium glazes	Cancer, lung and kidney disease. Avoid use.
Thermal	Burns (especially with Raku)	
Biological	Mold in stored moist clay bodies	Fungus infection of fingernails
	Mold in hay or straw	"Farmer's Lung" disease

What to Do

1. Design the work space for convenient storage, easy maintenance, and good ventilation, including a hood and exhaust fan for each kiln. Salt glazing must not contaminate downwind neighbors.

2. Store all glaze chemicals in closed containers, clearly labeled.

3. In order to minimize exposure to dusts, the mixing of large quantities of dry clays should be done in a space other than the work area and apart from other workers.

4. Handle glaze chemicals with extreme caution to avoid inhaling or carrying them on clothing, thus exposing infants or small children.

5. All spray glazing must be in ventilated booth.

6. Replace asbestos gloves with nonasbestos substitutes. Try to get talcs with low asbestos content (e.g., some California talc) and/or use clay bodies with no talc or low talc content.

7. Keep small children out of the work space. Supervise young children closely wherever ceramics materials are present.

8. Change school programs if ventilation is not adequate. If there is absolutely no alternative to using unvented electric kilns, fire after school hours. Do not use lead or lead frit glazes for school programs or for ceramic items that will hold food, and use elsewhere only if absolutely necessary.

9. Do not smoke or eat in work space.

10. Use a respirator approved for toxic dusts and localized ventilation while mixing clays and glazes in quantity. Remember that although the individual doing the mixing is protected others in the same room may not be.

11. Daily damp cleanup is essential.

12. Ask for accurately labeled products, particularly when buying for school programs.

13. Get pulmonary function test every 2–3 years.

14. Avoid cotton clothing when doing Raku, and wear protective, flame retardant clothing or covering. Keep area clear of loose combustibles. Have water or fire extinguisher. Avoid use of damp, moldy hay or straw.

15. Do preventive exercises to strengthen back. For carpal tunnel syndrome, use pug mill, learn to alter throwing style, and take 15-minute breaks while throwing or wedging to elevate hands (possibly with ice pack on wrists) and take pressure off wrists.

16. If fingernail infection occurs and doesn't heal, tell physician that it may be a fungus.

2. Collage, Decoupage, Assemblage

	Type of Exposure	Nature of Problem
Chemical	Adhesives	White glues and polyvinyl acetates (PVA) are relatively nontoxic. All others contain organic solvents that may degrease skin and affect nervous system, liver, etc., and are often flammable. Epoxies cause allergies.
	Paints, lacquers, varnishes, shellacs, and their thinners	Pigments in paints may cause heavy-metal poisoning. Solvents affect nervous system, liver, etc., and are often flammable.
	Polyurethane 2-part resin systems	Irritating to skin, eyes, lungs. Cause asthma.
What to Do	1. Use less toxic adhesives wherever possible and avoid spray forms. Avoid adhesives with benzene. 2. All paints, adhesives, pigments, thinners, etc., should be in closed storage. 3. Localized ventilation should be used for adhesives, paints, and other materials containing solvents or resins.	4. Wash exposed skin frequently. Wear protective clothes that are left in the studio. 5. Do not eat, drink, or smoke in work area. 6. Daily moist cleanup is necessary.

3. Dyes

	Type of Exposure	Nature of Problem
Chemical *(Note: Each dye has a color index number, which can be used to help identify what types of chemicals are present.)*	Direct dyes, including benzidine dyes, Cushing's Perfection, Dylon Multicolor, Keystone, Union, Putnum All Purpose, Rit, and Tintex	Caustic, irritate lungs, cause allergies and cancer of bladder
	Azoic, "Naphthol," "Ice Colors," "Fast Base," and "Fast Salt"	Skin problems
	Fiber Reactive, Procion, Procinyl, Procilan	Lung allergies
	Disperse dyes	Skin rashes, possibly cancer
	Acid dyes and basic dyes	Relatively harmless. May burn skin.
	Mordant and Natural Dyes	Major problems are from mordants, described below.
	Vat dyes, including indigo	See Mordants below.
	Oxidation base and aniline dyes	Can cause cancer
	Mordants:	
	Alum (potassium aluminum sulfate)	Rare skin and lung allergies. Generally low toxicity
	Copperas (ferrous sulfate, green vitriol)	Low toxicity
	Cream of tartar (potassium acid tartrate)	Nonhazardous
	Copper sulfate (blue vitriol)	Irritant to skin, mucous membranes. Acute and chronic internal effects
	Stannous (tin) chloride	Irritant to skin, eyes, gastrointestinal system

Type of Exposure	Nature of Problem
Oxalic acid	Caustic and corrosive to skin and on inhalation; highly toxic on ingestion
Acetic acid, vinegar	Even dilute acetic acid may be lung irritant and caustic to skin
Ammonia	Very irritating to skin, mucous membranes, respiratory system
Bleach, household (5% sodium hypochlorite)	Corrosive to skin, mucous membranes. Do not use to remove dye from skin. Do not mix with ammonia or acid; produces toxic gas.
Glauber's salt (sulfate salts)	Diarrhea, relatively low toxicity
Hydrosulfite, sodium (also called hyposulfite) hydrosulfite, color remover	Irritant, flammable, generates heat on contact with water
Potassium dichromate	Prolonged exposure may cause ulceration of skin, mucous membranes, perforation of nasal septum, and allergies
Tannic acid (oak galls, sumac leaves)	Slight skin irritant; otherwise generally nontoxic
Lye, caustic soda, sodium hydroxide	Extremely corrosive to all tissue; ingestion of $\frac{1}{3}$ ounce may be fatal to adults
Washing soda, sal soda, soda ash, sodium carbonate	Corrosive to skin, mucous membranes, gastrointestinal system
Beeswax and other waxes (when heated above 160°F, 71°C)	Fumes may cause acute and chronic respiratory irritation. Flammable.

What to Do

1. If possible, work in an area entirely separate from the living area. *Never* use the kitchen or kitchen utensils for dyeing.

2. Have closed storage of all dyes and mordants.

3. If possible obtain and keep dyes in liquid or paste form, rather than mixing powder.

4. Avoid direct, azoic, and oxidation base dyes.

5. Have localized exhaust ventilation for mixing and dyeing.

6. Wear protective gloves and work clothes that are kept separately and washed (separately from other laundry) often.

7. Use easily cleaned or disposable material on work surface and do daily moist cleaning.

8. Have water and eyewash readily available for emergency cleanup and treatment of caustic burns.

9. When mixing caustics put chemical into water, not vice versa, to avoid boiling up and splashing. Wear protective goggles when mixing caustics.

10. If mixing powder, use toxic-dust mask.

11. Heat wax in electric pan, and keep temperature to minimum necessary to melt wax. Have fire extinguisher available.

12. Do not eat, drink, or smoke in work area.

4. Fiber, Fabric, Basket Making

	Type of Exposure	Nature of Problem
Chemical	Dyes and mordants	See Studio Guide 3: Dyes
	Dust of cotton, jute, and, to a lesser extent, other vegetable fibers.	Cause acute lung irritation. Cotton fiber particularly causes chronic lung disease.
	Dust of synthetic fibers	Some contain formaldehyde residues, to which some people develop allergies.
	Wool, hair, and animal fibers	Allergies
Kinetic	Chronic back strain from poor sitting position, repetitive activities.	Weavers' Back
Biological	Anthrax bacteria from contaminated imported wool or hair.	Potentially fatal infection. *Rare in humans.*
	Fungus in basket materials	Fungus infections of fingernails.

What to Do

1. Daily moist cleaning of work surface and floor to limit airborne fibers is necessary.

2. Use localized exhaust ventilation for prolonged work with dusty materials. Even a floor loom can be set up with localized below-face-level ventilation.

3. If severely allergic to synthetic fibers, you may have to avoid these entirely. Desensitization is often possible for mild allergies to wool, hair, and animal fibers.

4. Do preventive exercises for back problems, get comfortable seating, and change position and activities every half hour.

5. Be alert to slowly healing wounds; these may be symptomatic of rare anthrax.

6. If soaking grasses, etc., change water daily to avoid fungus growth. If fingernail infection needs treatment, tell physician it could be fungus.

7. Get pulmonary function test every 2–3 years for frequent exposure to cotton dust.

5. Glassmaking

	Type of Exposure	Nature of Problem
Chemical	Free silica/sand, sandblasting	Silicosis of lungs
	Colorants: lead, arsenic, metallic compounds, and lusters	Heavy-metal poisoning
	Talcs	Contain asbestos. See Studio Guide 1: Ceramics
	Asbestos gloves, insulation	See Studio Guide 1: Ceramics
	Fiber glass, mineral wool	See Studio Guide 1: Ceramics
	Flocking fibers	Irritate lungs; cotton dust can cause permanent lung damage.
	Fuming, electroplating, etching, polishing	Gases and mists cause acute and chronic lung damage.
	Hydrofluoric Acid	Severe skin burns and lung damage.
Radiation	Ultraviolet light	Acute and chronic eye damage—cataracts

	Type of Exposure	Nature of Problem
Thermal	Burns	
	Stressful amounts of heat	Heart and kidneys overworked and may collapse. When a person works in high heat for at least two hours a day for five days, the body adjusts itself to a stressful situation, making subsequent periods of exposure less stressful. This acclimatization lasts two months beyond the end of the exposure, so glassworkers who have become adjusted to high heat can take a vacation and not lose their acclimatization. Acclimatization, however, produces a variety of harmful reactions such as skin disorders, water and salt imbalance, heat exhaustion, cramps, edema. Heat stress can also cause discomfort, irritation, and reduced efficiency of physical and mental work, with increased error rate and more injuries. Heat syncope—giddiness, fatigue, and fainting—is warning to avoid further exposure. At this point, the body's capacity to adjust is seriously limited and death may result.

What to Do

1. Plan work and storage areas to reduce airborne dusts. Use closed storage for all liquids and colorants. Hydrofluoric acid requires special containers as recommended by supplier.

2. Make sure that there is adequate exhaust and dilution ventilation in work areas, particularly for "fuming," etching, grinding, and electroplating operations.

3. Do daily wet mopping and cleaning of work area.

4. Use protective clothing in high-temperature areas, preferably wool or leather. Cotton is more likely to burn. Do not wear synthetic fabrics, which can melt and adhere to the skin.

5. Wear well-fitting, sturdy shoes, preferably safety pull-on type with no laces to catch hot sparks or fragments.

6. Replace asbestos gloves with new nonasbestos heat-protective gloves.

7. Use specially designed protective lenses to reduce ultraviolet exposure.

8. Remove asbestos-containing substances wherever possible and substitute other insulating materials.

9. Try to obtain talc with low asbestos content (e.g., some California talc). If iron impurities are no problem for aesthetics of work, use Vermont talc, which has iron but no asbestos. (This is the talc used for baby powder.)

10. Interrupt long work sessions with occasional breaks in cool, fresh air. Have adequate salt and fluid intake.

11. Do not eat, smoke, or drink in the work area.

12. Have fire extinguisher available, as well as a cold-water source for treatment of burns.

6. Cold Glass, Stained Glass, Lampwork

	Type of Exposure	Nature of Problem
Chemical	Lead fumes in soldering, dust in filing and machining	Lead poisoning. New studies indicate even low blood levels are harmful.
	Fluxes	Lung and mucous membrane irritation
	Acids in etching	Burns, vapors irritating to lungs and mucous membranes.
	Hydrofluoric acid	Severe burns and lung irritation
	Cyanides	Fatal poison in minute amounts
	Solvents	Damage to nervous system, liver, etc.
	Synthetic resin adhesives	Allergic reactions
	Silver compounds, solutions and electroplating	Stain and irritate skin
	Grinding	Abrasives can cause silicosis and some allergies
	Flocking fibers	See Studio Guide 5: Glassmaking

What to Do

1. Supply work areas with good exhaust ventilation drawing contaminated air away from workers' breathing zones and supplying fresh, clean air. Production workshops or areas in constant use require appropriate ventilation systems designed for specific operations.

2. Plan work area to isolate leadworking and etching from other activities.

3. Reserve work cloths for work area. Change shoes when leaving work area to avoid tracking lead dust.

4. Use closed storage for all materials. Hydrofluoric acid requires storage in specially constructed containers as recommended by supplier.

5. Daily wet cleaning of work area is necessary.

6. Have a good sink and running water near acid operations. For schools and production workshops, a body shower and eyewash fountain should be available.

7. Use protective gloves and aprons when using solvents, acids, resins.

8. Never eat, drink, or smoke in work area.

9. Children and pregnant women should not be exposed to lead or solvents.

10. A person who works regularly with lead should have blood tests every few months. No amount of lead is considered safe. If tests show over 30 micrograms/100 ml., ventilation, housekeeping, and protective clothing are inadequate and need to be improved. Avoid further lead exposure until tests return to normal and environmental corrections have been made.

7. Leatherworking

	Type of Exposure	Nature of Problem
Chemical	Dyes, mostly direct	See Studio Guide 3: Dyes. Solvents are a problem.
	Solvents	Skin degreasing and irritation, nervous system and liver damage, flammable
	Organic dusts from leather	Dermatitis, lung irritation
	Cements, glues, resins	Skin allergies, effects of solvents
Kinetic	Cuts and lacerations	
Biological	Skins, hair	Rarely, anthrax. Mostly from imported materials

What to Do

1. Secure local exhaust ventilation for work with dyes, cements, burning tools.

2. Use protective gloves for work with stains, dyes, cements, oils, waxes, other finishes.

3. Wash hands frequently.

4. Reserve work clothes for work area.

5. Use closed storage for dyes, solvents, glues, and resins.

6. Do damp cleaning of work area daily.

7. Do not eat, drink, or smoke in the work area.

8. Keep children out of the work area when solvents or dyes are in use.

9. Be suspicious of sores that heal slowly, a possible indication of anthrax.

8. Metals: Fine Jewelry and Foundry

	Type of Exposure	Nature of Problem
Chemical	Silver and gold	No major problems
	Copper, zinc, bronze alloys, plastics	Fumes cause flu-like symptoms several hours after exposure, which last about 24 hours. This is most likely if you have had no exposure for several days. Known as zinc shakes, welders fume fever, plastic fume fever, etc. No long-term effect. Also occurs occasionally with many other metals.
	Cadmium and cadmium solders	Fumes extremely toxic, causing both acute and chronic lung disease and kidney disease.
	Beryllium	Serious acute and chronic lung disease, ulcerations.
	Scrap or "found" metals	May contain mercury antifouling compounds that can cause mercury poisoning
	Colorants: metallic, etc.	Vary widely in toxicity, but assume all are capable of heavy-metal poisoning
	Nickel Carbonyl (for molds)	Causes both acute respiratory and other effects and cancer of lung and nose.
	Bone	Allergic reactions to dust
	Pickling compounds	Burn skin, irritant to lungs and mucous membranes
	Mold materials: silica sand, silica flour, French chalk (talc), investment-casting plaster	Silicosis of lungs. Asbestos in talc
	Resins	Lung allergies

	Type of Exposure	Nature of Problem
	Styrofoam decomposition products	Acute lung and skin irritation
	Wax	Acute lung and mucous membrane irritation, flammable
	Solvents and degreasers	Dermatitis, nervous system and liver damage, flammable
	Cutting oils	Dermatitis, acne, lung disease, falls due to slippery floors
	Glues and epoxies	Skin allergies, solvent effects
	Grinding and buffing compounds	Dermatitis; wheels may contain silica and formaldehyde resins, causing silicosis and lung allergies
	Soldering	See Studio Guide 9: Metals: Welding, Brazing, Soldering
	Asbestos insulation	Lung disease and cancer
Kinetic	Grinding and buffing	Danger of injury from work that flies out or gets caught. Especially a problem with students who have not been taught the proper handling of the operation.
	Hammering	Noise leading to deafness; vibration affecting circulation in hands
Thermal	Soldering	Burns
	Hot pickle Baths	Burns
Biological	Bone	Rarely, anthrax

What to Do

1. Provide closed storage (flame resistant, where appropriate) of solvents and degreasers, colorants, mold materials, buffing compounds, pickling materials.

2. Have localized ventilation for pickle baths, etching, solvents, soldering, buffing. Ventilation systems for buffing wheels, if properly designed, may recover several hundred dollars of salable silver and gold dust annually.

3. If possible, avoid use of cadmium, beryllium, nickel carbonyl. Find substitutes for asbestos, benzene, and carbon tetrachloride.

4. Do daily damp cleanup of work area.

5. No eating, drinking, or smoking in studio.

6. Have water supply for emergency treatment of chemical or other burns and fire extinguisher handy.

7. Be suspicious of wounds or sores that heal slowly if working with bone.

8. Keep separate work clothing in studio.

9. Use goggles for buffing, grinding, pickling, and soldering.

10. Wash hands frequently when working with colorants, glues, buffing, pickles, and solvents.

11. Ear protection for hammering and other noisy procedures.

12. Students need specific instruction in methods for buffing and grinding before they start this activity.

For Foundries, the following must also be considered:

13. Small foundries require specialized planning for ventilation and control of air contaminants. Guidelines can be found in the American Foundrymen's Society's *Engineering Manual for Control of Inplant Environment in Foundries* (see Appendix 4: References).

14. If dust levels are high or toxic materials are being used, wear appropriate respirators.

15. Use protective gloves, face shield, aprons, and nonflammable (specially treated) pure cotton or wool clothing. Synthetic fibers melt, causing complicated burns.

16. Wear special safety shoes that slip on and off easily and have no laces or opening into which molten metal could splash. "Lace-boot burns" are common in foundries. When hot metal splashes into conventional boots, it is impossible to remove the boot before serious burns take place.

17. Damping of trip hammers to reduce noise and vibration.

18. Covering of belts, pinch points, hammer activation controls, etc., in keeping with OSHA requirements to prevent crushing, amputations, and similar serious injuries.

19. If you are using cutting oils, you should clean the floor regularly to reduce slipperiness and fire hazard. Skin care is necessary to prevent dermatitis and acne.

20. Have hearing tested every 2–3 years.

9. Metals: Welding, Brazing, Soldering

	Type of Exposure	Nature of Problem
Chemical	Metals that cause fume fever.	See Studio Guide 8: Metals: Fine Jewelry and Foundry
	Cadmium, beryllium, nickel	See Studio Guide 8: Metals: Fine Jewelry and Foundry
	Lead solders and alloys	Lead poisoning
	Painted or scrap metals	Paints may contain lead, and scrap metals may have mercury antifouling compounds.
	Welding rods	Contain 40 combinations of metals, rarely labeled as to content, with varying toxicities. Cadmium, in particular, may cause fatal toxicity.
	Fluoride	Hydrofluoric acid is extremely corrosive to lungs, skin, etc.
	Chromic acid	Causes cancer, ulceration of skin, lung irritation.
	Acetylene gas	Mild narcotic effect. May have more toxic contaminants.
	Nitrogen dioxide (arc welding)	Lung irritation
	Ozone (from ultraviolet radiation). Ultraviolet effect on degreasing compounds in welding area.	Lung irritation. Forms highly toxic phosgene gas.
Thermal	Burns and Fire	

Radiation	Ultraviolet, produced in arc welding	Burns skin and eyes, causes fatigue. Inert-gas-shielded welding is the most hazardous.
	Infrared	Can cause burns, headache, eye damage. In some industries 50% of the arc welders have eye irritation, 25% have cornea damage.

What to Do	1. Know your equipment and materials; follow safety instructions exactly.	6. Never weld in an area where solvents, degreasing, or other cleaning processes are present.
	2. Use required protective clothing of leather or wool and equipment such as gloves and goggles or hoods.	7. Have water for emergency decontamination of acid spills or splashes and fire extinguishers available.
	3. Welder protective lenses to avoid radiation damage to eyes are essential.	8. Get pulmonary function test every 2–3 years.
	4. Be sure the ventilating system functions; check it periodically while you work.	9. Separate flammable materials and welding process by 35 feet unless protective wall is between them.
	5. Never work in confined spaces without ventilation, air-supplied respirators, or self-contained breathing equipment.	

10. Painting and Drawing

Type of Exposure	Nature of Problem
Paints (fingerpaint, water colors, tempera, oil, latex) and pigments	As with glazes, all pigments and colorants should be presumed to be capable of producing toxicity unless they have been specifically certified as nontoxic by The Art and Craft Materials Institute. The carriers for paints, however, vary widely in toxicity from non-toxic water, to toxicity from fungicide in some latex paints, and the considerable toxicity of the organic solvents in all oil-base paints.
Medium: denatured alcohol, hydrochloric acid, vinyl-butyl resins.	Damage to liver and other organs. Some are skin irritants.
Filler: diatomaceous earth (celite), silica, mica (silicate)	Frequent exposure to dust may cause silicosis.
Grounds: flake white and other lead compounds	May cause lead poisoning. Avoid use without strict control.
Paintbrush cleaners may contain aromatic hydrocarbons, methyl alcohol (methanol), acetone	Acute and chronic nervous system and liver damage, some can cause cancer. Most are flammable.
Paint and varnish removers and stripping compounds may contain:	
Methylene chloride	Produces carbon monoxide, which may cause heart failure if ventilation is not excellent.
Cresols	Irritate skin; can cause liver damage.
Phenols	Can irritate or penetrate the skin. May cause liver damage.

Alkalis	Prolonged exposure causes skin and/or lung irritation.
Chalk, charcoal, pencils, artists' pastels	See Pigments above. Dusts are probably not encountered in amounts large enough to cause serious problems, with possible exceptions of pastels containing toxic pigments.
Artists' varnishes containing driers or siccatifs (metallic salts), solvents	Solvents are dangerous to nervous system and liver, and are flammable.
Inks: drawing or India, fluorescent, indelible, stamping; and gels, extenders, cleaners	Contain ingredients toxic in varying degrees if swallowed. May contain organic solvents that, if inhaled in large quantities, could produce effects of other solvent exposures. Absorption of dye chemicals through skin is a potential hazard. If label says flammable assume solvent is organic. However, nonflammable material may contain chlorinated hydrocarbons.
Epoxy compounds	Irritate skin, cause lung allergies
Polyurethane and polyurethane compounds	Prolonged inhalation may cause skin, eye, and lung irritation.
Aerosol spray propellants: fluorocarbons (freons), propone	Highly volatile; except at high concentrations, usually only mildly irritating to respiratory tract and eyes.
Fixatives: atomizer spray with alcohol content	Probably not hazardous in conventional use.
Marking pens with permanent ink containing aromatic hydrocarbons.	Prolonged use causes headaches or nausea, irritates lungs, and possibly damages liver.
Marking pens with water-based ink.	A problem only if dye is ingested.

What to Do	**1. Plan for and use a good ventilation system that will allow for a supply of clean, fresh air. Studio exhausts should not be recirculated in an air-conditioning system.**	**2. Maintain good housekeeping practices. Use disposable paper under work surfaces and discard after working. Damp wipe work surfaces daily.**

3. Wear a smock or other covering over clothing and launder it frequently.

4. Use substitute materials and processes if discomfort develops in the presence of a particular substance, such as turpentine.

5. Cover containers of solvents when they are not in use. Evaporation takes place continuously, increasing as the temperature goes up. (Brushes standing in solvents will add to this evaporation.)

6. Dispose of solvent-soaked papers or rags quickly. Special storage cans for this purpose are needed to prevent leakage of vapors.

7. Keep all solvents off the skin as much as possible. If skin contact is made, wash immediately with soap and water and replace skin oils with a lanolin or other cream.

8. Do not eat, smoke, or drink in the work place. Wash hands before you handle food and utensils or use the toilet.

9. Do not put paintbrushes or other working tools in the mouth or near it.

10. Use spray materials or tools only in spray booths with an appropriate respirator.

11. Papermaking

	Type of Exposure	Nature of Problem
Chemical	Cotton linters, other fibers	All are safe in wet form. Cotton dust can cause chronic lung disease. Jute and sisal dust irritate lungs and occasionally cause pneumonia.
	Lye (sodium hydroxide)	Extremely caustic to skin, eyes, lungs
	Sodium hypochlorite (bleach)	Caustic to skin. Releases acutely toxic gas in presence of ammonia or acid.
	Colorants	See Studio Guide 3: Dyes
	Sizing, stiffeners, e.g., gums, resins, polyvinyl alcohol, Hercules 40, rice and wheat flours	Most are basically harmless. Canada balsam and acetyl cellulose use flammable solvents.
	Lead, silver, bismuth, and other impregnators	Heavy-metal poisoning
	Plaster of Paris	Nuisance dust
	Liquid latex	Ammonia causes acute irritation to eyes and lungs.
	Fixative sprays	Irritating to lungs. Contain organic solvents.
	Thymol mold inhibitors	Mildly toxic

What to Do

1. Closed storage is needed for caustics, thymol, latex, colorants, and impregnating materials.

2. Periodic cleanup if dust accumulation is a problem.

3. Fixative spraying should be done in a well-ventilated area. Because of irritating effects, latex molds probably should also be made with good ventilation.

4. Caustics should be mixed by adding caustic to water, not vice versa, and using with protective clothing and goggles, with water and eyewash available for emergency flushing of spills.

5. Never mix sodium hypochlorite with ammonia or acid.

6. There should be no eating, drinking, or smoking in the studio.

7. See Studio Guide 3: Dyes, for precautions in use of these.

12. Photography

Type of Exposure	Nature of Problem
Most chemicals mentioned in this chart can cause skin and lung irritation on short-term exposure and severe skin and lung allergies after prolonged use. Persons with preexisting allergies may be more vulnerable. Several chemicals are absorbed through both skin and lungs.	
Developers: includes catechin, hydroquinone, monomethyl P-aminophenol sulfate, phenidone, potassium bromide, pyrogallic acid, sodium carbonate, sodium sulfite	Most harmful are catechin and pyrogallic acid. Least harmful (although not innocuous) are phenidone and sodium sulfite.
Stop baths: acetic acid and chrome alum	Highly irritating to skin and lungs on both acute and repeated contact.
Fixing baths: acetic acid, alum, ammonium thiosulfate, boric acid, hypo (sodium thiosulfate)	Acetic acid and thiosulfates are the major problems; the latter release sulfur dioxide gas on heating or exposure to acid.
Intensifiers: ammonia, hydrochloric acid, mercuric chloride and iodide, potassium bromide, potassium chlorochromate, potassium cyanide, potassium dichromate, silver and uranium nitrate	All but potassium bromide are extremely irritating and/or corrosive on skin, inhalation, or ingestion. Potassium bromide is moderately harmful through these routes. Potassium cyanide is highly toxic in even small amounts.
Reducers: ammonia persulfate, hypo, iodine, potassium cyanide and ferricyanide (Farmer's reducer), potassium permanganate, sulfuric acid	Most are irritating or caustic. Hypo, ammonium persulfate, and potassium ferricyanide can release highly toxic gases on exposure to heat or acid. Potassium cyanide is toxic in small amounts. Ferricyanide is not a problem except as described above.

Type of Exposure	Nature of Problem
Toners: ammonium and ferric alum, gold and platinum chloride, potassium oxalate, potassium sulfide (sepia toner), sodium sulfide, oxalic acid, selenium oxide, thiourea	All can cause various degrees of skin irritation and most can cause damage through inhalation. Potassium and sodium sulfide and selenium oxide release highly toxic gases on contact with acid. Least harmful are the alum and thiourea.
Hypo eliminators: hydrogen peroxide, ammonia potassium permanganate, bleaches, potassium persulfate	Hydrogen peroxide is safest. Others are irritating or corrosive or release toxic gases on contact with heat.
Film cleaners: may contain ammonium hydroxide, chlorinated solvents, methyl alcohol, trichloroethane	These chemicals are listed as moderately to very toxic and may have serious effects, particularly in aerosol form. Methanol vapors are known to cause irritation of respiratory tract leading to bronchitis. Heavy exposure may cause trembling, intoxication, blurred vision. Absorbed through skin.
Propellants such as freon and other fluorocarbons	Highly volatile; except at high concentrations, usually only mildly irritating to respiratory tract and eyes.
Formaldehyde	Highly irritating and often causes severe allergies on contact with skin and through inhalation. May cause cancer.
Methyl chloroform	Mildly irritating to skin, causes CNS depression and liver damage. On contact with hot surfaces creates deadly phosgene gas.
Bleach (sodium hypochlorite)	Irritating to skin. Forms toxic gas on contact with acid or ammonia
Color processing	Most color processes cause skin and respiratory damage or allergies. Some also cause liver damage, birth defects, etc. P-phenylene-diamine and tertiary-butylamine borane are absorbed through skin. Sulfamic acid releases toxic gas on exposure to heat or acid.

What to Do

Everyone who works with photographic chemicals should have a basic understanding of the nature of the chemicals and their interaction with one another. Photographers should learn the art and the chemistry of photography at the same time.

1. Always provide exhaust ventilation in close proximity to chemicals in use and a fresh air source for the darkroom. All mixing of chemicals should be done under localized ventilation.

2. Plan the darkroom carefully for good storage and efficient work patterns to reduce unnecessary handling of and exposure to chemicals. All chemicals, including baths, should be covered when not in use.

3. Wipe up all spills and splashes promptly; dispose of rags and papers contaminated with chemicals in closed containers.

4. Use aerosol-spray products only in a spray booth or with efficient exhaust ventilation.

5. Avoid skin contact with chemicals by using protective gloves or tongs. If you must put your hands in chemicals, wash them immediately afterwards.

6. Launder work clothing frequently. Wash hands well before eating, smoking, or using the toilet.

7. Do not smoke, eat, or drink in the darkroom.

8. Keep small children, asthmatics, and persons with other chronic respiratory diseases out of darkrooms.

9. Use complex color-developing processes, obsolete methods, or new technologies cautiously. Many new chemicals have not been tested, and little is known about their toxicity. Obsolete methods were frequently discarded because they were unsafe.

10. For laser use, special protective eyewear is needed, as is proper shielding of equipment. See Appendix 4: References, for materials providing specific information.

13. Plastics

	Type of Exposure	Nature of Problem
Chemical	In general, plastics that are being created from monomers and polymers that are being heated or machined (creating vapors or dust) should be treated as if they can cause lung and skin allergies or acute and chronic effects on the central nervous system, liver, and blood forming organs. In rare cases plastics such as vinyl chloride may cause cancer. Many of the materials involved are also highly flammable.	
	Acrylic resins, plexiglas, lucite, methyl methacrylate (sometimes with hydroquinone as stabilizer)	Nervous system effects, allergic reactions of skin and lungs. With heat, plexiglas forms methyl methacrylate.
	Ethylene dichloride and methylene chloride cements used with acrylics	Cause problems similar to those of the acrylics. Contain organic solvents
	Styrene monomer, and polystyrene foam when heated above 480°	Irritation of eyes, nose, and throat, nausea, dizziness, fatigue. Foam releases methyl chloride on sawing large slabs of fresh material, which can damage nervous system, liver, kidneys, and bone marrow.
	Materials used with polyester or styrene resins:	
	Methyl ethyl ketone peroxide, other organic peroxides	Irritating to skin, mucous membranes, eyes; prolonged inhalation of vapors results in headache, throat irritation. Effects may be cumulative. Any splash of MEK peroxide in eyes can cause blindness. Explosive

Accelerators: cobalt naphthenate, dimethyl aniline	May cause contact dermatitis, which may appear five or more days after first use or nor until after years of exposure. Dimethyl aniline is absorbed through skin.
Inhibitors: tertiary butyl catechol, hydroquinone	Repeated exposure may cause anemia. Easily absorbed by skin; may cause damage to central nervous system and/or circulatory system.
Polyethylene (pellets used for fusing at oven temperatures around 300°F, 154°C, in injection molding)	Monomer released in heating and carbon monoxide released in burning are probably not serious problems in quantities used by artists.
Polyurethane foam, foaming constituents:	
Toluene di-isocyanate (TDI) and other di-isocyanates	May cause irritation to skin, eyes, respiratory tract; may cause allergic bronchial asthma
Diphenyl methanocyanate	Irritating to skin, less toxic than above
Decomposition (pyrolysis) products begin at 325°F, 163°C, in hot-wire cutting or burning	Toxic vapors contain small amounts of cyanide gas
Dusts in sawing, cutting	Lung irritation, inflammation; eventual scarring has been found in animal studies.
Vinyls, sprayable compounds used in sculpture:	
Polyvinyl chloride	Decomposition products include HCl gas and plasticizers.
Polyvinyl esters, polyvinyl alcohol, -acetyls, -ether, polyvinylidene chloride	Skin irritants
Toluene	Toxic. See Solvents, Chapter III, Tables II and III
Amino and phenolic resins in foundry work (used as binders in shell molding, during forming and machining processes) contain formaldehydes (urea-, malamine-, phenol-) and cashew-shell.	Dermatitis, irritation to eyes, throat, and respiratory tract. Decomposition of these resins begins at 350°F, releasing ammonia, formaldehyde, carbon dioxide, and some hydrogen cyanide, with extreme irritation of eyes, throat, and lungs.

Type of Exposure	Nature of Problem
Epoxy resins and hardeners become volatile during mixing, handling, curing of putty, gels, and liquids	Skin and lung allergies; corrosive to skin
Dusts and vapors of hardened resins during machining, finishing operations	Allergic symptoms involving skin and lungs
Fillers used with liquid plastics are part of the dusts created in machining and finishing resin forms: diatomaceous earth (celite), silica flour, mica, other silica-containing substances	Add to toxicity of resin dusts. Silica-containing materials can cause silicosis of lungs.
Sawdust, chopped natural fibers	May cause allergy
Asbestos	Cancer causing, should never be used. Find substitute
Fiber glass	Acute lung and skin irritation; so far believed to be only a nuisance dust
Solvents:	
Methyl ethyl ketone	Moderate toxicity
Diacetone alcohol	Good odor warning. Irritates eyes and mucous membranes. May cause drowsiness, possible damage to kidneys and liver.
Methylcyclohexanone	May cause irritation, discomfort, possible narcotic effects.
Cellosolve, butyl cellosolve	Both absorbed through skin. Toxicity of butyl cellosolve is greater than cellosolve.
Plasticizers:	
Dibutyl phthalate	Little toxic effect found

Tricresylphosphate, triorthocresylphosphate	Skin irritant. Absorbed through skin and causes severe nerve damage.

What to Do

1. Avoid working with liquid resins near living areas.

2. Do not eat or smoke while working.

3. Do not allow children to use these materials or to be present in work areas while they are being used.

4. Provide exhaust ventilation for the work site. Exhausted air should not be recirculated. Production shops that routinely use foaming or vacuum-forming operations must have professionally planned ventilation.

5. Avoid skin and eye contact by wearing specified gloves, goggles, apron, and clean, uncontaminated, or disposable clothing. Discard torn gloves. Wash clothing after each use.

6. Cover work areas and floors with paper. Dispose of contaminated paper in tightly covered container.

7. Use air-supplied respirator for all spraying and other work with uncured resins and components unless ventilation is very good. Filtering respirator is useful only for work on a very small scale.

8. Wash well with soap and water before eating, drinking, and using the toilet. Replace natural skin oils with lanolin cream.

9. Pay particular attention to fire-resistant storage, avoid open flame, sparks, and excess heat, and have a fire extinguisher available.

10. Instruct all persons coming into contact with plastic components in the safe use and handling of these materials.

14. Printmaking

Type of Exposure	Nature of Problem
Inks contain solvents, oils, pigments (including lampblack), driers, diazo powder (condensation product of formaldehyde and diazodiphenyl-amine)	See Solvents, Chapter III, Tables II and III. Many pigments can be toxic by ingestion, as are driers containing compounds of metals such as cobalt, lead, and manganese. Lampblack and other coal-tar derivatives can cause skin cancer.
Solvents in ink, lacquers, as cleaners, diluents, etc. Particularly hazardous because of the nature of their use: spread over wide areas during cleaning operations and on machinery during printing, often simultaneously in a single area	See Solvents, Chapter III, Tables II and III. Pregnant women are at particular risk in working with organic solvents or substances containing such solvents. Organic solvents, such as used for silkscreening, are more of a problem than are linseed-based materials.
Acids:	
Nitric, hydrochloric, potassium chlorate, iron perchloride	Highly corrosive in full strength. Vapors may do serious lung damage requiring medical assessment. Effects on lungs may not become apparent until several hours after exposure. Dilute acids are less toxic, although prolonged inhalation or skin contact may be harmful. Iron perchloride is safest of group.
Potassium dichromate	Highly corrosive to skin. Repeated inhalation of low concentrations can result in ulceration and perforation of nasal septum. Some people develop allergies to dichromate.
Sulfuric, all except dilute strength	Acts rapidly; exposed skin must be washed immediately with copious amounts of water.
Acetic	Vapors irritate lungs, can produce bronchial constriction.

Phosphoric, oxalic, tannic	Adverse effects are not common, but avoid unnecessary exposure. Phosphoric acid can cause serious burns.
Talc dust	Frequently contaminated with asbestos, which is dangerous to breathe. Talc sold for baby powder is asbestos-free.
Bronzing powders, pigments such as diazo dye powders, resin	Probably not hazardous to health in amounts used in printmaking, but avoid unnecessary exposure. Grounds are flammable, and aquatint boxes are explosive.
Asphaltum	Skin irritant. Prolonged exposure in industry more hazardous. Flammable

What to Do

Printmaking studios, laboratories, shops, and presses require planned localized ventilation. In the development of new facilities, artists should participate in planning with architects and ventilation engineers to be sure that their needs are understood and met.

Printmakers who work independently or in improved spaces should get professional assistance to plan safe ventilation if possible. Guidelines for installation of hoods and fans are given in *Industrial Ventilation: A Manual of Recommended Practice* (see Appendix 4: References).

1. Do not eat, drink, or smoke in the work area.

2. Minimize skin contact with chemicals by wearing gloves and apron. Change work clothes frequently. Use polyvinyl alcohol gloves with solvents and neoprene or butyl rubber gloves and aprons with acids.

3. Wear an appropriate respirator for short-term operations if ventilation is inadequate.

4. If possible, substitute water-based silkscreen inks for organic-solvent-based ones.

5. Keep work area clean, free from dusts or spilled chemicals. Do daily moist cleanup. Materials used to clean spills must be kept in closed containers.

6. Have access to running water for immediate washing of acid spills, and to an eyewash fountain, if possible.

7. Areas where flammable materials, especially grounds and aquatint boxes, will be used or stored must be spark free. See: Moses, *Health and Safety in Printmaking,* in references (Appendix 4).

15. Woodworking

In contrast to the major problems of the other mediums, those facing the woodworker involve safety and avoidance of lacerations, amputations, and fires, rather than long-term threats, such as development of chronic diseases. But, although issues of safety may be more serious than those of health, the latter also are important.

	Type of Exposure	Nature of Problem
Chemical	Wood and wood dusts	Studies are just beginning to show that prolonged exposure to wood dust results in a mild degree of chronic lung disease. Woodworkers do have an increase in cancer of the nasal sinus; the overall incidence is estimated at 2.5% of workers after an average delay of 40 years or more. Therefore, other health and safety issues are of more immediate importance. Several imported hardwoods and a few native woods (e.g., redwood and western red cedar) do cause direct contact allergies to skin and/or inhalation allergies to lungs.
	Dusts of compounds in or on woods: fillers, adhesives, stains, finishes, oils, wax, insecticides, preservatives	May include synthetic resins that irritate and sensitize. Other chemicals can cause allergic reactions and possibly more serious effects after prolonged exposure.
	Fumes from scorching or melting wood fillers and/or adhesives during machining, sawing	Add to irritant effects of dusts
	Bleaches may contain acids or caustics	Lung and skin irritants
	Stripping compounds:	

	Methylene chloride	Forms carbon monoxide, which affects oxygen-carrying capacity of blood, and may cause heart failure in susceptible individuals.
	Methanol (wood alcohol)	Ingestion and inhalation can cause blindness and liver damage. Some absorption occurs through skin.
	Paints, varnishes, stains, etc.	See Studio Guide 10: Painting and Drawing
	Solvents	See Solvents, Chapter III, Tables II and III. Flammable; affect nervous system and lungs
Kinetic	Dust, chips	Irritations from dusts, injuries from larger particles
	Noise of saws and other machinery	Fatigue and annoyance, hearing loss
	Vibration	Repeated blows or prolonged use of vibrating tools like chain saws can cause conditions called "dead" or "white" fingers, in which normal circulation is impaired and numbness occurs. Can be disabling if stress continues.

What to Do

1. Develop and use exhaust ventilation for each dust- or vapor-producing operation.

2. Train everyone who works with potentially hazardous wood materials and processes in proper and safe methods for handling tools. *Do not remove guards on machinery.*

3. Wear hardware-store-type dust masks only for temporary dust protection.

4. Use barrier creams or appropriate gloves to prevent skin absorption of solvents and other chemicals. These measures will also prevent irritation and sensitization by chemicals that are not absorbed by the skin.

5. Paint removers and strippers may contain very hazardous chemicals. Use exhaust ventilation in all operations involving vats of these substances, or work outdoors. These materials must be kept in closed storage and used with protection against fire and with fire extinguishers available. Cloths for spills and cleaning should be placed immediately in covered containers to prevent further leakage into the air.

6. Wear goggles and other protective clothing and use a respiratory device when work is prolonged. Use ear protection—muffs or stoppers—for excessive noise.

7. Use tools with comfortable handles. Keep hands warm. Rest often when using vibrating tools and when chipping or chiseling for long periods.

Appendixes:
Getting Additional Information

1. Poison Control Centers

Region	Where to Call for Help	
		The centers listed below have been certified as regional centers by the American Association of Poison Control Centers. These centers can often provide information about the contents and/or acute (not chronic) toxicity of brand-name and generic products either for preventive purposes or in an emergency. This list was correct as of January 1983.
New England	Massachusetts Poison Control System 300 Longwood Ave. Boston, MA 02115 617-232-2120 800-682-9211 (MA only) 617-277-3323 (Hard of Hearing)	
Middle Atlantic	Long Island Poison Center Nassau County Medical Center 2201 Hempstead Turnpike East Meadow, NY 11554 516-542-2323	New York City Poison Center Department of Health Bureau of Laboratories 455 First Ave. New York, NY 10016 212-340-4494 212-764-7667

Finger Lakes Poison Center LIFE LINE
University of Rochester Medical Center
Rochester, NY 14620
716-275-5151
717-275-2700 (Hard of Hearing)

South	National Capital Poison Center Georgetown University Hospital 3800 Reservoir Rd. Washington, D.C. 20007 202-625-3333 Georgia Poison Control Center Grady Memorial Hospital 80 Butler St., S.E. Atlanta, GA 404-588-4400 800-282-5846 (GA only) 404-525-3323 (Hard of Hearing)	Maryland Poison Center University of Maryland School of Pharmacy 636 W. Lombard St. Baltimore, MD 21201 301-528-7701 800-492-2414 (MD only)
Midwest	Central and Southern Illinois Poison Resource Centers 800 E. Carpenter Springfield, IL 62702 217-753-3330 800-252-2022 (IL only) Indiana Poison Center 1001 W. Tenth St. Indianapolis, IN 46202 317-630-7351 800-382-9097 University of Iowa Hospital Poison Information Center Iowa City, IA 52240 319-356-2922 800-272-6477 (IA only)	Southeast Regional Poison Center Children's Hospital of Michigan 3901 Beaubien Detroit, MI 48201 313-494-5711 800-572-1655 Western Michigan Regional Poison Center 1840 Wealthy S.E. Grand Rapids, MI 49506 616-774-7854 800-632-2727 (MI only)

Hennepin Poison Center
Hennepin County Medical Center
701 Park Ave.
Minneapolis, MN 55415
612-347-3141

Children's Mercy Hospital
24th at Gillham Rd.
Kansas City, MO 46108
816-234-3000

Cardinal Glennon Memorial
Hospital for Children
1465 S. Grand Ave.
St. Louis, MO 63104
314-772-5200
800-392-9111 (MO only)

Mid Plains Regional Poison Center
Children's Memorial Hospital
8301 Dodge
Omaha, NE 68114
402-390-5400
800-642-9999 (NE only)
800-228-9515 (surrounding states)

Southwest

Arizona Poison and Drug Information Center
Arizona Health Sciences Center
University of Arizona
Tucson, AZ 85724
602-626-6016
800-362-0101 (AZ only)

New Mexico Poison, Drug Information, and Medical
Crisis Center
University of New Mexico
Albuquerque, N.M. 87131
505-843-2551
800-432-6866 (NM only)

Southeast Texas Poison Center
University of Texas Medical Branch
8th and Mechanic Sts.
Galveston, TX 77550
713-765-1420

Rocky Mountain

Rocky Mountain Poison Center
Denver General Hospital
W. 8th Ave. and Cherokee Sts.
Denver, CO 80204
303-629-1123
800-332-3073

Intermountain Regional Poison Control Center
50 N. Medical Dr.
Salt Lake City, UT 84132
801-581-2151

Sacramento Medical Center
2301 Stockton Blvd.
Sacramento, CA 95817
916-453-3692
800-852-7221 (Northern CA only)

San Diego Regional Poison Center
University of California at San Diego Medical Center
225 W. Dickinson St.
San Diego, CA 92103
619-294-6000

San Francisco Bay Area Regional Poison Control
Center
Room E86
San Francisco General Hospital
1001 Potrerro Ave.
San Francisco, CA 94102
415-666-2845
800-792-0720

Children's Orthopedic Hospital and Medical Center
4800 Sandpoint Way, N.E.
Seattle, WA 98105
206-634-5252
800-732-6985

Deaconess Hospital
W. 800 5th Ave.
Spokane, WA 99210
509-747-1077
800-572-5842

2. Some Sources for Protective Clothing and Equipment

Acme Products, Scott Aviation
Division of "Automatic" Sprinkler Corp. of America,
1201 Kalamazoo St.
South Haven, MI 49090

Bausch and Lomb, Inc.
P.O. Box 478
Rochester, NY 14602

E.D. Bullard Co.
2680 Bridgeway
Sausalito, CA 94965

Direct Safety Co.
7815 South 46 St.
Phoenix, AZ 85040

W.W. Grainger, Inc.
General Offices
5959 W. Howard St.
Chicago, IL 60648
(141 locations throughout U.S.)

Lab Safety Supply Co.
P.O. Box 1368
Janesville, WI 53547

Mine Safety Appliances Co.
201 No. Braddock Ave.
Pittsburgh, PA 15208

Minnesota Mining and Manufacturing Co.
2501 Hudson Rd.
St. Paul, MN 55101

Pulmosan Safety Equipment Corp.
30-48 Linden Pl.
Flushing, NY 11345

Check under Safety Equipment and Clothing in the Yellow Pages of your phone directory for local suppliers.

3. OSHA (Occupational Safety and Health Administration)

Regional Offices

Region I
16-18 North St.
1 Dock Square
Boston, MA 02109
Telephone (617) 223-6172

Region II
Room 3445, 1 Astor Plaza
1515 Broadway
New York, NY 10036
Telephone (212) 944-3432

Region III
Gateway Building
3535 Market St.
Philadelphia, PA 19104
Telephone (215) 596-1201

Region IV
1375 Peachtree St. NE
Suite 587
Atlanta, GA 30367
Telephone (404) 881-3573

Region V
230 S. Dearborn St.
32nd Floor, Room 3244
Chicago, IL 60604
Telephone (312) 353-2220

Region VI
555 Griffin Square Bldg.
Room 602
Dallas, TX 75202
Telephone (214) 767-4731

Region VII
911 Walnut St., Room 406
Kansas City, MO 64106
Telephone (816) 374-5861

Region VIII
Room 1554, Federal Building
1961 Stout St.
Denver, CO 80294
Telephone (303) 837-3061

Region IX
P.O. Box 36017
450 Golden Gate Ave.
11349 General Bldg.
San Francisco, CA 94102
Telephone (415) 556-0586

Region X
Federal Office Building, Room 6003
909 1st Avenue
Seattle, WA 98174
Telephone (206) 442-5930

4. References

Asterisks denote materials that are not so technical as others or are important, despite some technicality, for practical application and understanding.

Accident Prevention Manual for Industrial Operation. National Safety Council, 425 No. Michigan Ave., Chicago, IL 60611.

Air Sampling Instruments Manual, 2d ed., 1962. American Conference of Governmental Industrial Hygienists, 1014 Broadway, Cincinnati, OH 45202.

*Alexander, William C., 1973–74. "Ceramic Toxicology," *Studio Potter* (Winter), Box 65, Goffstown NH 03045.

All About OSHA: The Who, What, Where, When, Why, and How of the Occupational Safety and Health Act of 1970. Office of Information, OSHA, US Department of Labor, Washington, DC 21210. (Ask also for any updated material, since the Act has undergone recent changes and may undergo further changes.)

Alternatives for the Artist. A series of guides to the safe use of materials in ceramics, painting, photography, and printmaking (with more topics to follow) produced by the Health Hazards in the Arts Program of the School of the Art Institute of Chicago, Columbus Drive and Jackson Blvd., Chicago, IL 60603.

Art Hazards News. Excellent periodical on health issues available through $13 subscription from Center for Occupational Hazards, Inc. 5 Beekman St., New York, NY 10038

*Breysse, Peter A., 1972 ed. *Manual for Eye and Face Protection in Educational Institutions. Environmental Health and Safety News,* Vol. 20, Nos. 1, 2, 3, 4. University of Washington, Seattle, WA 98195.

*Carnow, Bertram W., 1974. *Health Hazards in the Arts and Crafts.* 5340 N. Magnolia St., Chicago, IL 61640.

*Cerone, G., 1983. "A Filtered Spray Booth," *Ceramics Monthly,* April, p. 52.

*Cutter, T., M. Clark, and J. McGrane, 1984. *A Ventilation Handbook for the Arts.* Center for Occupational Hazards, Inc. 5 Beekman St., New York, NY 10038.

Deichmann, W.F., and H.W. Gerarde, 1969. *Toxicology of Drugs and Chemicals.* New York: Academic Press.

*Eckhardt, R.E., and R. Hindin, 1973. "The Health Hazards of Plastics," *Journal of Occupational Medicine,* Vol. 15: pp. 808–19.

Elkins, H.B., 1959. *The Chemistry of Industrial Toxicology,* 2d ed. New York: Wiley.

*Encyclopedia of Occupational Health and Safety, 3rd ed, 1983. 2 vols. International Labor Office (Geneva), 666 11th St. NW, Washington, DC 20001.

Engineering Manual for Control of In-Plant Environment in Foundries, 1956. American Foundrymen's Society, Des Plaines, IL 60018.

Environmental Health and Safety News. Department of Environmental Health, School of Public Health and Community Medicine, University of Washington, 461 Health Sciences Building, Seattle, WA 98195.

Fairhall, L.T., 1957. Industrial Toxicology, 2d ed. Baltimore: Williams & Wilkins.

*Gosselin, R.E., et al., 1976. Clinical Toxicology of Commercial Products. Acute Poisoning, 4th ed. Baltimore: Williams & Wilkins.

A Guide for Uniform Industrial Hygiene Codes or Regulations for Laser Installations, 1968. American Conference of Governmental Industrial Hygienists, 1014 Broadway, Cincinnati, OH 45202.

Hamilton, Alice, and H.L. Hardy, 1974. Industrial Toxicology, 3d ed. Acton, MA: Publishing Sciences Group.

*Held, Robert, "Glass Studio." School of Design, Mississauga, Ontario, Canada.

*Hogan, Barbara, Dennis Darcey, Ann Janney, and Albert Fritsch, 1976. Aerosol Sprays. Center for Science in the Public Interest, 1757 S St., Washington, DC 20009. (Printing and Drawing.)

*Hricko, Andrea M., 1976. Working for Your Life: A Woman's Guide to Job Health Hazards. Labor Occupational Health Project, University of California, 2521 Channing Way, Berkeley, CA 94720.

*Hunt, W., 1978. "Frit Formulas," Ceramics Monthly, May, pp. 48–54.

Hunter, D., 1969. The Diseases of Occupations, 4th ed. Boston: Little, Brown.

*Hygienic Guide Series. American Industrial Hygiene Association, Hygienic Guides Committee, 25711 Southfield Rd., Southfield, MI 48075.

*Industrial Data Sheets. National Safety Council, 425 No. Michigan Ave., Chicago, IL 60611.

*Industrial Ventilation: A Manual of Recommended Practice, 14th ed., 1976. Committee on Industrial Ventilation. PO Box 16153, Lansing, MI 48902. American Conference of Governmental Industrial Hygienists.

Jacobs, M.B., 1949. The Analytical Chemistry of Industrial Poisons, Hazards, and Solvents. New York: Interscience.

The Job Safety and Health Act of 1970: Text, Analysis, Legislative History. Bureau of National Affairs, Washington, DC.

*Krochmal, Arnold, and Connie Krochmal, 1974. The Complete Illustrated Book of Dyes from Natural Sources. Garden City, NY: Doubleday.

*Labino, Dominick, 1968. Visual Art in Glass. Dubuque, IA: W.M.C. Brown

*Mayer, Ralph, 1970. *The Artist's Handbook of Materials and Techniques,* 3d ed. New York: Viking.

*McCann, Michael, 1975. *Health Hazards Manual.* Foundation for the Community of Artists, 220 5th Ave., New York 10003.

*McCann, Michael, 1979. *Artist Beware.* New York: Watson Guptill Publications.

*McDermott, H.H., 1979. *Handbook of Ventilation for Contaminant Control.* Ann Arbor, MI, Ann Arbor Science Publishers Inc.

*Moses, C., *et al.,* 1978. *Health and Safety in Printmaking.* Alberta Labour, Occupational Health and Safety Division, Occupational Hygiene Branch, 2nd floor, Oxbridge Place, 9820-106 St. Edmonton, Alberta T5K 2J6 Canada.

Nelson, Glenn C., 1960. *Ceramics: A Potter's Handbook.* New York: Holt, Rinehart & Winston.

Newcomb, B.C., 1984. "Eye Protections for Welders Need Right Lens Shade, Hardness," *Occupational Health and Safety,* February, pp. 34–36. Medical Publications, Inc. 5002 Lakeland Circle, Waco, TX 76710.

Occupational Diseases: A Guide to Their Recognition, 1964. U.S. Department of Health, Education, and Welfare, Public Health Service, Washington, DC. Public Health Service paper No. 1097.

Olishifski, J.B., and F.E. McElroy, eds., 1971. *Fundamentals of Industrial Hygiene.* National Safety Council, Occupational Health Series, 425 No. Michigan Ave., Chicago, IL 60611.

Patty's Industrial Hygiene and Toxicology, Vols. I–III, 3rd ed. 1978, 1979. New York: Interscience.

*Piepenburg, Robert, 1972. *Raku Potter.* New York: MacMillan.

*Planer, R.G., 1979. *Fire Loss Control: A Management Guide.* Marcel Dekker, Inc. 270 Madison Ave., NY.

Pyle, James L., 1974. *Chemistry and the Technological Backlash,* Chap. 5. Englewood Cliffs, NJ: Prentice-Hall. (Ceramics.)

Preventing Dermatitis If You Work with Epoxy Resins. U.S. Department of Health, Education, and Welfare, NIOSH, Washington, DC. Pub. No. 74-130.

Ramazzini, Bernardo, 1964. *Diseases of Workers,* trans. W.C. Wright. NY: Hafner.

Registry of Toxic Effects of Chemical Substances, 1976 ed. U.S. Department of Health, Education, and Welfare. Public Health Service, Center for Disease Control, NIOSH, Rockville, MD 20852. For sale by the Superintendent of Documents, U.S. Government Printing Office, Washington, DC 20402.

Respiratory Protective Devices Manual, 1963. American Conference of Governmental Industrial Hygienists, Committee on Respirators, 1014 Broadway, Cincinnati, OH 45202.

Rhodes, Daniel, 1957. *Clay and Glazes for the Potter.* Philadelphia: Chilton.

Sax, N.I., 1968. *Dangerous Properties of Industrial Materials,* 3d ed. New York: Van Nostrand Reinhold.

*Scatchard, T., 1983. "A Better Vent for Electric Kiln," *Ceramics Monthly,* December, pp. 34–35.

*Sering, R., and C. Steinberg, 1983. "Comment: Carpal Tunnel Syndrome," *Ceramics Monthly,* December, pp. 21–22, 62.

*Siedlecki, Jerome T., 1968. "Potential Health Hazards of Materials Used by Artists and Sculptors," *Journal of the American Medical Association,* June 24, pp. 1176–80. Reprints from Department of Occupational Health, American Medical Association, 535 No. Dearborn St., Chicago, IL 61610.

*Siedlecki, Jerome T., 1972. "Potential Hazards of Plastics Used in Sculpture," *Art Education,* February, pp. 21–26.

*Sliney, D., *Guide for Control of Laser Hazards—1981.* American Conference of Governmental Industrial Hygienists, 6500 Glenway Ave., Bldg D-5, Cincinnati, OH 45211.

*Stellman, J.M., and S.M. Daum, 1973. *Work Is Dangerous to Your Health: A Handbook of Health Hazards in the Work Place and What You Can Do about Them.* New York: Vintage.

Stemmer, Klaus L., *et al.,* 1975. "Pulmonary Exposure to Polyurethane Dust," *Environmental Health Perspectives.* June, pp 109–14 U.S. Government Printing Office, Washington, DC 20402.

Thomas, Charles C., T.T. Mercer, and P.E. Morrow, 1972. *Inhalation Studies with Freshly Generated Polyurethane Foam Dust.* Springfield, IL. p. 540.

Threshold Limit Values. Updated annually. American Conference of Governmental Industrial Hygienists, 1014 Broadway, Cincinnati, OH 45202.

*Untracht, Oppi, 1975. *Metal Techniques for Craftsmen.* Garden City, NY: Doubleday.

U.S. Environmental Protection Agency, 1976. *Investigation of Selected Potential Environmental Contaminants: Ketonic Solvents.* National Technical Information Service, Springfield, VA 22151. Document No. PB 252970.

Voss, W.A.G., 1970. *Advances in the Use of Microwave Power.* U.S. Department of Health, Education, and Welfare, Washington, DC.

Waldbott, George, M.D., 1973. *Health Effects of Environmental Pollutants.* St. Louis: The C.V. Mosby Company.

* Waller, J.A., 1980. "Another Aspect of Health Issues in Ceramics," *Studio Potter,* Issue No. 2, pp. 60–61, Box 65, Goffstown, NH 03045.

*Waller, J.A., 1984. "Studio Health and Safety: Striking a Balance Between Caution, Cost, and Safety," *Studio Potter,* Issue No. 2, pp. 62–66, Box 65, Goffstown, N.H. 03045.

*Waller, J.A., and L. Whitehead. A series of media-specific articles on woodworking, ceramics, jewelry, fiber arts, printmaking, metalsmithing, papermaking, and ventilation that appeared in *Craft Horizons* between June/July 1977 and December 1977/January 1978, and in *American Craft* from December 1979/January 1980 to December 1980/January 1981. Published by American Craft Council, 401 Park Ave S., New York, NY 10016.

The Welding Environment: A Research Report on Fumes and Gases Generated during Welding Operations, 1973. American Welding Society, 2501 7th St. NW, Miami, FL 33125.

**Welding Safely,* 1972. U.S. Department of Health, Education, and Welfare, NIOSH. Public Health Service Pamphlet No. HSM 72-10261.

*Williams, William A., 1975. *Accident Prevention Manual for Shop Teachers.* American Technical Society, 5608 Stony Island Ave., Chicago, IL 60637.

5. Additional Sources of Information

American Industrial Hygiene Association (AIHA)
66 S. Miller Rd.
Akron, OH 44313

American Medical Association:
Council on Occupational Health Publications List
Department of Environmental, Public, and
Occupational Health, American Health,
American Medical Association
535 N. Dearborn St.
Chicago, IL 60610

Art and Craft Materials Institute
715 Boylston St.
Boston, MA 02116
(Certifies nontoxic materials for use by children)

Center for Occupational Hazards, Inc.
Michael McCann, Executive Director
5 Beekman St.
New York, NY 10038

Through a joint project, COH and I wrote to all occupational-medicine specialists in the United States and Canada to find which ones are interested in health problems of artists. If you need to consult an occupational-medicine specialist for evaluation of a health problem, write to COH for names in your area.

Manufacturing Chemists' Association
1825 Connecticut Ave. NW
Washington, DC 20009

Medical Committee for Human Rights
Occupational Health Project
558 Capp St.
San Francisco, CA 94110

National Safety Council
425 N. Michigan Ave.
Chicago, IL 60611

State Health Departments usually have units concerned with occupational and/or environmental health and can often be of considerable assistance. In all but the largest cities or counties, local health departments are less helpful.